Overcoming Anxious Attachment

Learn to Trust Others Fearlessly, Break Free from Childhood Wounds, and Develop Healthy Relationships Without Nagging Self-Doubt

Avery Parker

Contents

Introduction

Three years ago, during a particularly rough patch in my relationship, I sat in my bedroom, staring at my phone. Five hours had passed since I texted my partner, and my anxiety was skyrocketing with each passing minute.

Was I being too clingy?

Did I say something wrong?

These nagging doubts weren't new; they were my ever-present companion, an anxious attachment that controlled my emotional state and eroded my self-confidence. One sleepless night, I realized something had to change—not just for my relationships but for my own peace of mind.

This book is born out of that moment of clarity. It is a practical guide designed to help you, the reader, overcome the agony of anxious attachment because I know how it feels. As someone who has struggled with anxious attachment myself, I know the pain of trying to navigate relationships while battling anxiety and questioning everything. Together, we'll work on eliminating the insecurities that haunt your relationships and healing the deep-seated attachment wounds from your past, helping you regain your rightful self-confidence.

We'll begin by laying down the foundations of attachment theory, unraveling the 'why' behind your feelings. But we won't stop at theory. We'll delve into practical, actionable strategies that have proven effective in transcending anxious attachment for me and countless others. This book weaves personal anecdotes, scientific research, and a step-by-step guide to help you finally overcome anxious attachment and move forward with a healthier, secure attachment style.

As I moved towards a more secure attachment style, I learned that building healthy relationships is not easy, but it has been profoundly rewarding. I now wish to share this story with you, not as an expert talking down from an ivory tower but as a fellow traveler who has navigated the bumpy terrain of anxiety and insecurity stemming from anxious attachment yet found a secure partner who loves me and supports me in my healing.

This book is written with hope, understanding, and encouragement, mirroring a conversation with a trusted friend who understands because they've been there. As we proceed, I invite you to read and engage actively with the content. Reflect on your current attachment style and relationship dynamics. The purpose of this book isn't just about consuming information; it's about transforming your life.

By the end, you will understand anxious attachment and have a clear path to healthier, more secure relationships. Let's begin this transformative journey together. Where we start is less important than where we are going, and the promise of where we are going is a place of confidence, security, and healthy, enduring relationships.

Foundations of Anxious Attachment

In the quiet corner of a local library, Avery and Alex found themselves engrossed in an unexpected conversation about their personal struggles with relationships. Avery, flipping through a psychology book, looked up at Alex, who had just finished sharing a story about waiting anxiously for a call that never came.

"You know, Alex, anxious attachment isn't just about worrying in relationships," Avery began, her voice carrying a hint of empathy. "It's this constant need for reassurance, this fear of abandonment that can really shape how we see ourselves and others."

Alex nodded, his gaze thoughtful as he recalled his own journey with attachment patterns. "Yeah, it's like always feeling on edge, right? Like you're waiting for the other shoe to drop."

"Exactly," Avery replied, her eyes reflecting a mix of understanding and determination. "For me, it started becoming clear in my early relationships. I remember this one time in high school…"

She paused, collecting her thoughts as memories from years ago resurfaced vividly.

"I was dating this guy, James," Avery continued, her tone carrying a hint of nostalgia tinged with unease. "He was sweet, but I constantly needed to know where he was and what he was doing. If he didn't text back right away, my mind would race with worst-case scenarios."

Alex leaned in, sensing the weight behind Avery's words. "It must have been exhausting," he remarked softly.

"It was," Avery admitted with a sigh. "I didn't realize then that it stemmed from deeper insecurities. My parents divorced when I was young, and my mom always seemed distant afterward. I think I grew up feeling like I had to fight for attention and love."

She traced patterns on the table with her fingertip, lost momentarily in thought. "James didn't understand why I needed constant reassurance," Avery continued, her voice tinged with vulnerability. "And when he couldn't meet those needs, I felt like I wasn't important to him. It became a cycle of me pushing for more closeness and him feeling overwhelmed."

Alex nodded knowingly, recognizing the familiar tug of wanting closeness but fearing it at the same time. "It's like you're always craving that connection, but it's never enough to quiet the doubts," he reflected.

"Exactly," Avery agreed, her eyes meeting Alex's with a shared understanding. "I realized later that I was projecting my fears onto my relationships, expecting them to fill a void I needed to address within myself."

Their conversation delved deeper into the nuances of anxious attachment—the insecurities, the need for validation, and the difficulty in trusting others fully. They discussed how childhood experiences like Avery's with her parents' divorce, could lay the groundwork for these patterns in adulthood.

"It's like we learn early on how to navigate relationships based on those early experiences," Alex remarked thoughtfully, swirling his coffee in his cup.

Avery nodded, her expression thoughtful. "But understanding it is the first step toward changing it," she said, her voice firm with conviction. "Through therapy and self-reflection, I've been learning to recognize when those old patterns surface and how to respond differently."

"That's inspiring," Alex replied, a smile tugging at his lips. "Knowing that change is possible gives me hope."

Leaving the library that day, Avery felt a renewed sense of purpose. Sharing her story with Alex had not only connected them on a deeper level but had also reaffirmed her commitment to helping others understand and overcome their own attachment challenges. With each step forward, she knew she was laying the groundwork for a future of stronger connections and emotional resilience.

―――――

I still shudder when I think back to that story of waiting by the phone. Is that something you can relate to? Well, that feeling, a mix of fear and discomfort, not just passing but profoundly shaping your perception of relationships, could be more than mere worry. It's an essential characteristic of anxious attachment—a style of interpersonal relationship dynamics deeply rooted in fears of abandonment and rejection. This chapter guides you through understanding the complexities of anxious attachment. From its psychological foundations to biological influences and how it differs from other attachment styles, we will delve into the full spectrum of what it means to be anxiously attached. By unraveling these aspects, you're laying the foundation for your journey toward healing and cultivating more secure, satisfying relationships.

1.1 The Anatomy of Anxious Attachment: A Deep Dive

What is Anxious Attachment?

Anxious attachment is characterized by a chronic sense of relationship insecurity, accompanied by a compulsive need for closeness and an acute fear of separation. It is like that clingy friend who texts, "Are we cool?" after every hangout. You know, the one who's always craving reassurance and freaking out over minor stuff? Yeah, that's an anxious attachment in a nutshell. If you find yourself constantly seeking reassurance from your partners, or if the thought of being alone triggers intense anxiety, you might be experiencing signs of this attachment style.

Daily interactions and relationships often reveal distinct signs of anxious attachment patterns. "Anxious attachment is a term used in psychology to describe a specific style of relating to others, characterized by a fear of abandonment, a need for constant reassurance, and a tendency to overreact to perceived threats to the relationship (Tatkin, S. (2012)." Recognizing these signs in oneself can be both a confronting and enlightening experience, paving the way for meaningful change.

Individuals with anxious attachment often report higher levels of emotional hypersensitivity and may react to perceived relational threats with significant distress. This behavior pattern is not just disruptive—it can erode relationships and personal peace over time, making understanding its roots and manifestations crucial for anyone looking to foster healthier connections.

Let's explore some of the most common symptoms and signs of anxious attachment in adults, providing real-life examples to help you identify similar patterns in your own behavior.

Historical Context

The concept of anxious attachment didn't just pop up out of nowhere.. It was first developed in the mid-20th century by British psychologist John Bowlby, who introduced attachment theory to explain the intense distress experienced by infants separated from their parents. Bowlby's student, Mary Ainsworth, later expanded on his work through her 'Strange Situation' studies, which identified different attachment styles, including secure, avoidant, and anxious attachment. These pioneering works laid the groundwork for understanding how early interactions with caregivers could influence relationship patterns far into adulthood. Over the decades, this theory has been validated through various studies and across different cultures. It has also been expanded to understand adult relationships, offering a strong framework for exploring individual attachment styles. This can help explain, for example, why you might feel on edge if your boo doesn't reply back to your texts right away.

It's in Your Genes, Baby

Anxious attachment isn't just about feelings; there's science behind it too. Turns out, your genes and brain chemicals play a part. Neuroscience research has shown that attachment styles can be linked to the functioning of specific neurotransmitters and hormones. For instance, the attachment hormone oxytocin, often dubbed the 'love hormone,' plays a pivotal role in bonding and can affect how secure or anxious one feels in a relationship. Variations in the receptor genes for oxytocin and serotonin—a neurotransmitter involved in mood regulation—have been associated with differences in attachment styles. These biological factors can predispose individuals to be more sensitive to relational cues and potentially more prone to anxious attachment, highlighting the complex interplay between our bodies and emotional experiences. We will discuss more about the science behind attachment in Chapter 3.

Comparing Attachment Styles: It's Complicated

Understanding anxious attachment becomes clearer when contrasted with other attachment styles. Unlike securely attached individuals who feel comfortable with intimacy and autonomy, those with anxious attachment crave closeness but remain vigilant and doubtful about their relationships. On the other hand, avoidant attachment is characterized by a discomfort with closeness and a preference for emotional distance, a stark contrast to the anxious style's pursuit of intimacy. The disorganized attachment style, marked by a lack of explicit attachment behavior, shows a mix of behaviors associated with both anxious and avoidant styles, often resulting from more severe developmental disruptions or trauma. These distinctions are crucial as they help in self-recognition and guide the therapeutic approaches that might be most effective for each style.

1.2 Childhood Roots: Tracing Back to Where It All Began

Early Relationships: The Foundation of Future Patterns

In my own life, growing up with a father who repeatedly let me down taught me early on that I needed to rely solely on myself as others could not always be trusted.

I will never forget the day that everything changed in how I perceived my father. I learned that it was actually his own issues which built up a pattern of neglect that would later inform my own adult relationships. I was only five years old when I first realized how unreliable my father could be.

It was a chilly afternoon, and I was sitting on a small wooden bench in the after-school program room, watching the clock with growing anxiety. Normally, my babysitter would pick me up, but she had the day off, and my dad was supposed to come get me. As the minutes turned into hours, my nervousness grew. The cheerful chatter of other kids dwindled as they were picked up one by one until I was the last child left.

My teacher tried calling my dad repeatedly, her frustration evident with each failed attempt. I could see the worry lines deepening on her forehead.

"Don't worry, sweetie, I'm sure he'll be here soon," she said, though her voice lacked conviction.

I felt a mix of emotions: confusion, fear, and a creeping sense of shame. What was I supposed to do? I was only a child, yet my father, the parent, had forgotten me. The realization hit me like a punch to the gut.

Finally, after what felt like an eternity, the door swung open, and my father walked in. He was three hours late. There was no apology, no remorse. Instead, he looked agitated.

"Well, I'm here now. That's all that matters," he snapped.

I remember the feeling of embarrassment washing over me, the shame of having to make excuses for him, even at such a young age. My teacher gave him a look that I couldn't quite interpret at the time, but now I know it was a mix of disappointment and pity.

That day was the first of many where he would repeatedly show up late (if he remembered at all), distracted by his hobbies and unable to cope. Each time, the same pattern repeated. He would arrive late or not at all, always with an excuse, never taking responsibility.

As the years went by, I learned to be self-reliant. I couldn't trust him to be there for me, so I stopped asking for his help. I felt like I had to be totally responsible, even as a child. His inability to be dependable became a constant in my life, shaping the way I viewed relationships.

Whenever anyone in my life showed even a hint of his patterns... irresponsibility, failing to follow through on their word, or not showing up when they said they would—I put up a wall. I couldn't afford to be let down again.

That first incident left a deep imprint on my mind, a reminder that I had to trust only in myself. The fear of being let down became a guiding force in my life, influencing my interactions and relationships for years to come.

These early experiences with caregivers are crucial as they form the blueprint for our relationships later in life. When caregivers are emotionally unavailable or inconsistent, the child may develop a heightened sense of anxiety about relationships, fearing abandonment or believing that they must cling to others to receive the love and attention they crave. This pattern can profoundly affect their approach to relationships, as they are always on high alert, worried that showing their true selves or expressing real needs might lead to rejection or disconnection.

Developmental Impact: Shaping Self-Perception and Emotional Growth

Fast forward to adulthood, and those childhood hang-ups aren't just memories—they're messing with your self-esteem and sense of worth. Ever catch yourself wondering if your partner's love is real or just a 'like' on Insta? That's the anxious attachment rollercoaster, my friend. The impact of these early attachment experiences extends far beyond childhood, influencing emotional development and self-perception through adolescence and into adulthood. For those raised with inconsistent emotional support, there can be profound effects on self-esteem and self-worth. The internal dialogue might echo, "Am I worthy of love only when I am needed or perform well?" This questioning can lead to a pervasive sense of insecurity, where self-worth is constantly contingent on the approval and presence of others. Emotional development in this context is often skewed toward hyper-vigilance in reading others' cues and an over-reliance on external validation instead of cultivating a robust, internal sense of self and confidence. The psychological landscape of someone with an anxious attachment style may be riddled with doubt and a persistent fear of being 'not enough,' which can hinder personal growth and lead to recurring problems in forming healthy, reciprocal relationships.

Intergenerational Transmission: The Cycle Continues

Anxious attachment can be a legacy passed down through generations, creating a cycle that perpetuates patterns of insecurity and fear-based behaviors in relationships. If a parent has unresolved attachment issues, their ability to provide consistent and nurturing care can be compromised. Based on their unresolved needs and fears, they might oscillate between smothering affection and withdrawn behavior. This parenting style, often influenced by the parent's experiences with their caregivers, sets the stage for the next generation to inherit similar attachment anxieties. It's not uncommon to hear someone reflect on how their parent's emotional unpredictability or overt anxiousness in relationships has shaped their expectations and behaviors in love and friendship. Recognizing this intergenerational transmission is not just crucial; it's empowering, as it highlights an individual's emotional patterns and a familial passage of relational blueprints that may need healing and reconfiguration.

Critical Periods: Windows of Significant Influence

There are specific windows during a child's development that are particularly pivotal in the formation and solidification of attachment styles. The first two years of life are critical, as this is when attachment to primary caregivers is established. During this period, the quality of care—how responsive, consistent, and emotionally available caregivers are—directly influences the child's attachment style. This is a crucial time, as it lays the foundation for the child's future relationships. Another significant period is early schooling, where children begin to navigate relationships outside the family unit. How they relate to peers, form friendships, and perceive themselves within these new social contexts can reinforce or challenge earlier attachment patterns. Adolescence is another critical period, marked by a quest for identity and greater independence from parents. How teenagers manage these developmental tasks while navigating their attachment needs can significantly influence their emotional trajectory into adult relationships. These stages are not just milestones but key moments that shape our understanding of relationships and ourselves.

These early and critical periods in development set the groundwork for how individuals view themselves and others in the context of relationships. Understanding these foundational experiences provides a clearer lens through which to view current attachment behaviors, offering valuable insights into why one might cling to or excessively seek reassurance from partners. As we continue to explore these dynamics, keeping these developmental influences in mind can illuminate paths toward healing and transformation, offering a beacon of hope for creating more secure and fulfilling relational patterns.

1.3 The Brain on Anxiety: Neurological Underpinnings of Attachment

Brain Structures

Within the complex network of the human mind, specific regions play crucial roles in our attachment behaviors, especially when these attachments are tinged with anxiety. The amygdala, known as the emotional center of the brain, becomes particularly active in those with anxious attachments, making them quick to perceive threats, leading to heightened emotional reactions. Conversely, the prefrontal cortex, which is responsible for reasoning and emotional regulation, often lacks sufficient control in anxious individuals. This imbalance can lead to overpowering feelings of anxiety and fear of abandonment characteristic of anxious attachment. This neurological setup explains the persistent unease in relationships and sheds light on why breaking free from these patterns can feel daunting. The brain's wiring deeply influences how we react to our loved ones, and understanding this can be a decisive step in beginning to change those reactions.

Stress Response System

Ever feel like even a message left unread triggers a full-blown panic attack? Blame your HPA axis—the brain's stress thermostat. The body's stress response system, in this way, is critical to anxious attachment. This system orchestrates the body's response to stress and can become overly reactive in individuals with anxious attachment. Usually, this system helps the body adjust to stressors by controlling the release of cortisol, commonly known as the stress hormone. However, in those with anxious attachment, this axis can be triggered too quickly and too often, particularly in situations perceived as threatening to personal relationships. For example, a simple delay in text message response or an offhand comment can activate this stress response, resulting in heightened cortisol levels that lead to anxiety and agitation. This physiological response can make everyday interactions fraught with tension and fear, as the body is constantly on alert, mistakenly interpreting these minor events as severe threats to personal safety and well-being.

Neuroplasticity

However, there is a silver lining in the form of neuroplasticity—the brain's remarkable ability to reorganize itself by forming new neural connections throughout life. Think of it as how your brain's not set in stone; it's more like Play-Doh you can mold with the right tools.This ability means that even deeply ingrained anxious attachment patterns are not set in stone. Neuroplasticity provides hope that individuals can reshape their brain's reactions to stress and attachment through consistent and targeted practices, leading to a more secure and less anxious attachment style over time. Practices like mindfulness meditation and structured emotional reflection, as well as cognitive-behavioral therapy, can rewire the brain's pathways, strengthening the prefrontal cortex's ability to modulate the amygdala's hair-trigger responses. This reorganization can help temper the intensity of the stress response system, making what once felt like overwhelming threats more manageable and less catastrophic.

Neurological Differences

Research on the brain function of individuals with different attachment styles has revealed significant neurological differences (Johnson & Greenman, 2006). For instance, functional MRI (fMRI) scans have shown that people with anxious attachment tend to have more activity in the parts of the brain involved in emotional processing and less in areas related to cognitive control. This starkly contrasts individuals with secure attachment, who typically show a more balanced neural activity that supports emotional responsiveness and regulation. These findings suggest that anxious attachment is not just a habit of thought or a pattern of behavior but a deeply embedded neurological trait. However, the practical implications of these differences are not just about identifying deficits; they're about recognizing opportunities for personal growth and development. By targeting these specific brain areas through therapy and brain-training exercises, individuals can cultivate a more secure attachment style, thereby changing their perception of relationships and fundamentally altering the brain structures that support these feelings.

Understanding the brain's role in anxious attachment reveals the profound influence of our early experiences and genetic makeup on our relationships. However, it also offers a glimmer of hope. By embracing practices that harness the brain's ability to change and adapt, known as neuroplasticity, individuals can begin alleviating the anxiety that has long colored their connections with others. This opens up the possibility for more secure and satisfying relationships, suggesting that change is possible and within our control.

1.4 Recognizing Anxious Behaviors in Daily Life

We've all been there, anxiously awaiting a text message response from a loved one with anxiety building at every passing moment. However, if you're prone to interpreting any delay as disinterest or rejection, you might be experiencing one of the hallmark signs of anxious attachment. This behavior is typically accompanied by a continuous need for reassurance from partners or friends about their feelings toward you.

Red Flags Ahead (Symptoms and Signs)

If you start to notice that a casual comment from someone or actions like friends canceling plans disproportionately upset you or make you worry about the stability of your relationships, these could be signs that you may be struggling with anxious attachment.

If you often feel that you're overreacting to minor issues but feel powerless to control your emotional response, take note of these signs as well. Know that these symptoms are not just limited to your perceptions; they can often manifest in physical symptoms as well such as restlessness, difficulty concentrating, or even sleep disturbances when relationship issues aren't resolved. To manage these symptoms, consider practicing mindfulness, engaging in self-soothing activities, and seeking professional help if needed.

Love Drama (Relationship Dynamics)

Anxious attachment profoundly affects relationship dynamics, often skewing them toward imbalance and instability. For instance, if you have an anxious attachment style, you might find yourself clinging to your partner, fearing that giving them space would lead them to drift away from you. This neediness can manifest as constant texts, calls, or the desire to spend every possible moment together, often disregarding your partner's need for space and individuality (Gulli, 2024)." Such dynamics can lead to a vicious cycle where the more you cling, the more your partner might pull away, validating your fears of abandonment and rejection, thus increasing your anxious behaviors. It's a precarious balance where your actions, driven by fear and insecurity, might push away the very person you desire to keep close.

Self-Sabotage

Ever start a fight over who left the toilet seat up? Or create drama where there was none? Yep, that's your brain's sneaky way of saying, "Hey, let's test if they'll stick around." It's like setting relationship booby traps, just to see if they'll survive the emotional minefield. Usually, we call this self-sabotage. This tendency is one of the most harmful effects of anxious attachment. It often stems from a deep-seated belief, albeit unconscious, that you don't deserve happiness or that all good things will eventually fall apart. For example, you might start an argument over something minor or create issues where there are none, driven by the subconscious expectation that the relationship will fail. This behavior can be baffling not just to your partners but to yourself as well, as it contradicts your conscious desires for stability and love. Understanding this pattern is crucial; it originates from a fear that by finding fault in your partner or creating turmoil, you can somehow control the pain of potential rejection or disappointment rather than being caught off-guard.

The Quest for Validation

Constantly seeking validation and approval from partners or potential partners is another significant indicator of anxious attachment. Compliments? They're your love language. Criticism? Cue the waterworks. If you find yourself excessively happy when receiving compliments or devastated by criticism, it might be a sign that your self-worth is too closely tied to how others perceive you. This need for validation often leads to people-pleasing behaviors where you might go to great lengths to satisfy your partner, sometimes at the cost of your own needs and happiness. This search for approval is driven by the belief that love and acceptance from others is conditional, based on your actions rather than your inherent worth.

Recognizing these behaviors in yourself is the first step toward understanding the impact of anxious attachment on your life. It's about observing without judgment, acknowledging these patterns, and gently steering yourself toward healthier ways of relating to others. As we continue to explore these themes, remember that change is possible. Realizing these patterns is not an endpoint but the beginning of a path toward deeper self-awareness and, ultimately, more secure and fulfilling relationships.

1.5 Attachment Styles: A Spectrum of Relationships

Attachment styles are often presented in distinct categories: secure, anxious, and avoidant. However, human emotions and relationships are seldom that black-and-white. Instead, imagine attachment styles as existing on a broad spectrum, where individual experiences, personalities, and life circumstances combine uniquely to influence how we relate to others. This perspective allows us to appreciate our attachment styles' nuances and fluid nature, acknowledging that they can evolve and shift over time.

Understanding attachment as a spectrum rather than fixed categories opens up a more forgiving and flexible approach to self-perception and interactions with others. For instance, you might predominantly exhibit anxious attachment traits, such as needing frequent reassurance in relationships, yet display secure attachment qualities in your comfort with emotional intimacy and enjoyment of close relationships. This blending of styles can vary significantly from one relationship to another and can shift over time. Personal growth, healing from traumas, and positive relationship experiences all contribute to this fluidity. A person who once felt insecure in their attachments might gradually, through supportive relationships and personal development, find themselves feeling more secure and less driven by anxiety in their connections.

Moreover, the idea of mixed attachment styles is more than just a theoretical concept; it is a reality for many. It's not uncommon to find someone who exhibits traits of both anxious and avoidant styles, sometimes referred to as the fearful-avoidant attachment style. Here, individuals might deeply crave closeness and intimacy but fear being too dependent or close, leading to a push-pull dynamic in relationships. This complexity can make relationships challenging, as mixed signals and fluctuating needs can confuse partners and individuals. Recognizing this complexity is crucial in fostering self-understanding and patience, both with oneself and in interactions.

The influence of one's predominant attachment style extends deeply into how one selects partners and navigates relationship dynamics. People are often drawn to partners who confirm their beliefs about relationships. For instance, someone with an anxious attachment style may subconsciously choose a partner who is somewhat distant or inconsistent with their attention, thereby reaffirming the person's belief that they need to fight for love and that partners are unreliable. This pattern can perpetuate a cycle of dissatisfaction and insecurity in relationships. However, by understanding these tendencies, one can start to make different choices. They may seek more consistently supportive and responsive partners, which can help shift their attachment style toward a more secure model over time.

This dynamic interplay between our attachment styles and relationship choices highlights the importance of awareness and intention in managing our close connections. By understanding the spectrum of attachment styles and recognizing their fluidity, we can better navigate the complexities of love and relationships. We can choose partners who support our growth toward security and satisfaction rather than those who reinforce our fears and insecurities. This understanding empowers us to break cycles of unhealthy relationships and build stronger, more fulfilling connections that reflect our actual needs and desires.

As we reflect on this spectrum and its impact on our lives, consider how your experiences and growth has influenced your attachment style. Think about the partners you choose and the dynamics in your relationships. Are they reinforcing old patterns or helping you grow into the kind of attachment that feels healthy and secure? This reflection is not about judgment but about gaining clarity and making empowered choices in our relationships and emotional lives.

Identifying Personal Attachment Style

The sound of waves gently crashing against the shore provided a calming backdrop as Sophia walked along the sandy beach, her feet sinking slightly with each step. She held a book in one hand and a straw hat in the other, looking for a peaceful spot to settle down. In the distance, she noticed a figure sitting alone on a blanket, gazing out at the ocean.

As she got closer, she recognized James, a familiar face from the beach who often spent his weekends there. He seemed lost in thought, his eyes fixed on the horizon. Sophia decided to approach him.

"Hey, James," she called out, waving her hand. "Mind if I join you?"

James turned and smiled, his face lighting up with recognition. "Sophia! Of course, please do."

She spread out her blanket next to his and sat down, placing her hat beside her. "How have you been? You look deep in thought."

James sighed, running a hand through his hair. "I've been okay. Just thinking about some stuff—mainly relationships and why they always seem to get complicated for me."

Sophia nodded, her interest piqued. "I can relate. I've been reading about attachment styles lately, and it's been really eye-opening. Have you ever heard of them?

James shook his head. "Not really. What are they?"

Sophia leaned in, eager to explain. "Attachment styles are patterns in how we connect with others, especially in intimate relationships. They can explain a lot about our behaviors and feelings. There are four main types: secure, anxious, avoidant, and disorganized."

James looked intrigued. "Tell me more."

"Secure attachment means you're comfortable with intimacy and independence," Sophia began. "Anxious attachment involves a lot of worry about your relationships and needing constant reassurance. Avoidant attachment means you tend to distance yourself emotionally, and disorganized attachment is a mix of both anxious and avoidant behaviors."

James listened intently, nodding along. "That sounds really insightful. How can someone figure out their attachment style?"

Sophia reached into her beach bag and pulled out a printout. "I have a quiz here that helps identify your attachment style. I took it myself, and it was pretty revealing. Want to give it a try?"

James accepted the printout, curiosity evident on his face. "Sure, why not?"

They spent the next few minutes going through the quiz together. James answered each question honestly, reflecting on his past relationships and how he typically responded in various situations. After finishing, he handed the paper back to Sophia.

Sophia glanced at his results and smiled. "It looks like you have some anxious attachment traits. That means you might often feel insecure in relationships and need a lot of reassurance."

James nodded slowly. "That makes sense. I always thought it was just me being too emotional or needy."

Sophia reassured him. "It's not just you. Understanding your attachment style is the first step to improving your relationships. I've been working on mine, too. Recognizing these patterns can help us develop healthier ways of connecting with others."

James looked hopeful. "So, what can I do to change this?"

They continued their conversation, delving deeper into their personal experiences and how understanding their attachment styles could lead to more fulfilling connections. As the sun began to set, casting a warm glow over the beach, Sophia and James found comfort in their shared journey of self discovery and growth.

———

In personal growth and emotional well-being, identifying your attachment style is akin to navigating your way through a forest. It requires awareness, acceptance, and the courage to delve into the less-trodden paths of your emotional experiences. This chapter is designed to be your compass, guiding you through the intricate pathways of your attachment tendencies and helping you understand how they play a pivotal role in shaping your interactions and relationships.

2.1 The Attachment Style Quiz: A Personal Journey

About the Quiz

To kick off this exploration, I've included a quiz crafted by experts that acts like a mirror, reflecting your attachment patterns through the choices and reactions you show in various relationship scenarios.This quiz isn't just a set of questions; it's a journey into your relational psyche, designed to unearth the often subtle manifestations of your attachment style. The importance of approaching this quiz honestly can't be overstated—only with sincere responses can you gain the insights necessary for meaningful change.

Question Design

Each quiz question has been crafted by experts* to reveal your attachment dynamics by simulating relationship scenarios. For instance, if asked about your reaction to delayed messages from someone you're dating, your response can uncover patterns indicative of anxious or avoidant behaviors. These insights, grounded in psychological research, help pinpoint your attachment style—anxious, secure, avoidant, or a combination—offering a clearer view of your emotional tendencies.

Self-Assessment

As you take the quiz, trust your instincts and take a moment to ponder your feelings and responses. This introspection is key. For example, if relationship uncertainty prompts you to seek frequent reassurance, this may signal anxious attachment. On the other hand, distancing yourself to cope with discomfort suggests avoidant tendencies. Recognizing these patterns offers valuable insights into your interpersonal dynamics and emotional management strategies.

Scan the following QR code to access the following attachment style quiz and after viewing your results, feel free to return back here for more guidance.

All done? Upon completing the quiz, it is important not to see these results as rigid labels but as starting points for a deeper journey of personal growth and exploration. These findings give you a glimpse into your predominant attachment style, laying down a foundational framework that empowers you to delve into the nuances of your emotional world.

2.2 Interpreting Your Quiz Results: What It Means for You

Now, take a look at your quiz results and think about what your results mean to you. These quiz insights are valuable insights to your relationship puzzle, guiding you toward deeper self-awareness and harmonious relationships.

So, if your quiz points toward secure attachment, it shows you navigate relationships with resilience and adaptability, maintaining healthy boundaries even in challenges. It suggests a strong foundation to enhance your relational skills or support others toward secure attachment.

But, if your quiz indicates anxious attachment traits, it marks a crucial first step in understanding your relationship dynamics. Anxious attachment often stems from a fear of abandonment, driving a constant need for reassurance. This can create emotional highs and lows, intensifying dependence on others at the expense of your own well-being. Despite challenges, those with anxious attachment often exhibit strong empathy, nurturing deep connections when managed healthily.

We will discuss strategies for dealing with anxious attachment traits in later chapters. However, for severe cases impacting daily life, consider seeking professional help, particularly from therapists versed in attachment theory. Therapy offers a safe space to explore the root causes of anxiety, triggers, and strategies for building healthier relationships. Seeking help is a proactive step toward a more balanced, fulfilling relational life.

By embracing these insights, you address anxious attachment symptoms, fostering a compassionate self-relationship that enhances interactions with others. This journey shifts toward relationships as sources of growth and joy, not anxiety and fear.

2.3 Understanding Your Relationship DNA

When contemplating the dynamics of your relationships, it's important to acknowledge the foundational roles of both your genes and early environment. I refer to this unique interplay as your 'relationship DNA.' This concept encapsulates the intricate balance of your genetic predispositions and the environmental influences that collectively shape your connection and bonding with others. For instance, research in behavioral genetics suggests that while our genes influence our temperamental tendencies toward anxiety or sociability, the environment in which we grow up—whether it's stable and nurturing or inconsistent and chaotic—can significantly modify these genetic inclinations. This interplay ultimately determines how securely or anxiously we attach to significant others.

Understanding your relationship DNA is crucial because it provides insights into the deeply ingrained patterns that drive your relationship behavior. This self-awareness is the first step toward transformative growth. It allows you to see the threads that weave through your interactions and gives you the power to question whether these inherited patterns serve your well-being or hinder your relational satisfaction. For example, suppose you grew up in a home where caregivers were emotionally unavailable. In that case, you might find yourself drawn to similar dynamics in adulthood, not because they are healthy, but because they feel familiar.

The types of partners you find yourself attracted to and the relationship dynamics that ensue also speak volumes about your attachment style, which is a part of your relationship DNA. Often, without conscious awareness, people replicate familiar emotional environments. Suppose your attachment style leans toward the anxious. In that case, you might find yourself drawn to partners who are either overly nurturing—because they soothe your deep-seated fears of abandonment—or, paradoxically, to those who are dismissive because they echo the emotional unavailability you experienced in childhood. These attractions are not coincidences but guided by the underlying scripts written early in your life. By examining these patterns, you can begin to understand the qualities you are drawn to and the relationship dynamics they create. This awareness allows you to make more conscious choices in partners, gravitating toward relationships that foster security and growth rather than perpetuating cycles of anxiety and dissatisfaction.

Breaking these deeply ingrained cycles requires intentional action. It starts with the acknowledgment of your attachment style and its origins. From there, strategies such as mindful relationship choices, therapy, and continuous self-reflection become tools for rewriting your relational script. For instance, actively choosing to date someone who consistently demonstrates reliability and openness can gradually help reshape your expectations of relationships, teaching you that emotional availability and security are desirable and achievable. Additionally, engaging in therapies like Cognitive Behavioral Therapy (CBT) or Dialectical Behavior Therapy (DBT) can provide practical techniques to manage anxiety and reshape your relational responses. These therapeutic approaches help create new neural pathways that support healthier attachment behaviors, allowing you to rewire parts of your relationship DNA that no longer serve you.

Moreover, breaking these cycles isn't just about altering who you choose to be with; it's also about transforming how you show up in relationships. Developing a secure attachment style often involves:

- Learning to communicate your needs more clearly and assertively.
- Setting boundaries.
- Cultivating self-esteem that isn't reliant on external validation.

Each step in this process builds on the last, creating a cascading effect of positive change that improves your romantic relationships and enhances how you relate in friendships and professional connections. As you embark on this transformative process, remember that each slight shift contributes to a more significant evolution in your relationship DNA, steering you towards more nurturing, stable, and fulfilling interactions.

2.4 How Your Attachment Style Affects Your Relationships

In the intricate dance of human relationships, your attachment style wields significant influence, subtly shaping interactions across diverse relational landscapes—from romantic relationships to familial bonds and workplace dynamics. For those grappling with an anxious attachment style, this influence manifests vividly and often presents significant challenges.

Remember earlier when we were talking about that sinking feeling you get when you're eagerly anticipating your partner to call or text you back? You're eagerly anticipating your partner's call, but as the minutes tick by without a word, anxiety creeps in like an unwelcome guest. Thoughts whirl, imagining worst-case scenarios of abandonment or neglect. This hyper-sensitivity to perceived threats which may truly only be imagined, can make you feel like you're riding a rollercoaster of emotions, swinging between intense need for reassurance and profound fear of rejection.

These emotional highs and lows can strain the bedrock of any relationship—trust. Constantly questioning motives or overanalyzing actions can sow seeds of doubt and suspicion, corroding the very foundation needed for intimacy to thrive. And when it comes to setting boundaries, anxiously attached individuals may struggle, often prioritizing their partner's needs at the expense of their own, leading to imbalance and dissatisfaction.

Beyond romantic relationships, anxious attachment can cast its shadow over friendships and family dynamics. The quest for closeness might translate into clinginess or an overwhelming need for approval, potentially suffocating the very connections meant to nurture and support.

Even in professional settings, anxieties can surface, coloring interactions with colleagues and superiors. Feedback given may trigger defensiveness or an insatiable craving for reassurance, which can hinder growth and foster a perpetual sense of insecurity.

This happened in my own life, believe it or not. Even though many years have passed since then, I still vividly remember that fateful day.

I was twenty-one years old, fresh into the working world after graduating college at my first job (after spending the previous six months since graduating trying to get a job in my chosen career field). As they say, I was excited, bright-eyed, and bushy-tailed, going to work each day trying to learn and do my best. But it wasn't so long after that I quickly learned that my best wasn't good enough.

"Come in, please," my manager at the time had said, motioning towards the chair opposite her desk. As I entered her office that Friday afternoon, the weight of anticipation settled heavily on my shoulders. I could feel my palms start to sweat as she closed the door behind me.

"Thanks," I managed, trying to keep my voice steady despite the growing knot in my stomach.

"Let's talk about your recent work," she began, her tone measured but serious. "There have been some concerns."

Over the past weeks, I'd received feedback on every draft I submitted, always needing revisions. The uncertainty gnawed at me. During our last business trip, she'd hinted that this conversation might happen.

"I've been trying my best," I blurted out, my words rushed and tinged with desperation.

"That's what concerns me," she replied, her expression unreadable. "It seems you're struggling to meet our expectations."

My heart sank. This was it—the moment I'd feared. The words hung in the air, hitting me with a force I hadn't expected.

"I'm afraid we have to let you go," she concluded, her voice firm.

I felt a lump form in my throat. Tears threatened to spill over, and I fought to maintain composure. My mind raced back to my mom's advice: 'You can't cry at work.'

Blinking back tears, I nodded silently, struggling to process the suddenness of it all.

Now, those weren't the exact words, but I remember the message that rang through in my anxiously attached mind; that I wasn't good enough. Unfortunately, that message stuck with me for years. That nagging voice in the back of my head at the time felt like a slap in the face as if the world was saying, "Welcome to the Real World, Kid. It's tough out here." Over the following years, going through the struggle of continuing through various workplace challenges, from finding managers who cared or making enough to live comfortably without fear (spoiler alert: that didn't happen in New York City), I didn't know it at the time. Yet looking back now I can see how my anxious attachment kept me from trusting fully in myself. It also left me with damaging thoughts from the trauma such as: 'Is this really how the work world is going to be? I can't dare to make a mistake or rock the boat, or else I may be fired again.' Those debilitating thoughts could quickly escalate to a point where I regularly catastrophize about my worst fears - of becoming homeless - coming true.

Understanding these complex relational dynamics unveils a critical truth: your attachment style isn't just a facet of your personality—

it's a compass guiding how you navigate life's connections. Recognizing its presence across different spheres empowers you to embark on a transformative journey of self-discovery and growth.

By acknowledging and addressing the patterns of anxious attachment, you pave the way toward fostering relationships grounded in trust, mutual respect, and emotional resilience. This journey isn't just about unraveling old wounds but about embracing new possibilities for enriching and fulfilling connections that nurture your well-being and happiness.

2.5 The Role of Self-Esteem in Attachment Styles

The intricate dance between self-esteem and attachment styles, particularly anxious attachment, is akin to a feedback loop where each influences and sustains the other. Low self-esteem can often exacerbate the fears and behaviors associated with anxious attachment, such as clinginess and irrational fears of abandonment. This occurs because, fundamentally, self-esteem is about how much you value yourself—your sense of worth independent of external validation. When your self-esteem is low, you might find yourself constantly looking for signs that others value you, which can translate into an anxious need for constant reassurance in relationships. This neediness, in turn, can strain relationships, potentially leading partners to withdraw, thereby reinforcing the original fear of abandonment and further depleting self-esteem.

Conversely, improving your self-esteem can directly influence your attachment style, moving it toward more secure patterns. Recognizing and affirming your intrinsic worth makes you less dependent on others for emotional sustenance. You're more likely to engage in relationships from a place of wanting rather than needing, which fundamentally alters the dynamics of those relationships.

Relationships become less about seeking constant validation and more about mutual growth and joy. This shift can reduce the frequency and intensity of the anxious behaviors typical of anxious attachment, as the fear of abandonment diminishes with the understanding and internalization that being alone does not equate to being unworthy.

Building self-esteem, therefore, is beneficial and transformative, particularly for those with an anxious attachment style. This process begins with self-awareness—recognizing the negative self-talk and irrational beliefs perpetuating low self-esteem. For instance, replacing thoughts like "I must be loved by all to be worthy" with "My worth is inherent and not contingent on external validation" can start to shift your perception of self-worth. Furthermore, engaging in activities that reinforce a positive self-image, such as pursuing hobbies that you excel in or volunteering, which can provide a sense of accomplishment and purpose, are practical ways to enhance self-esteem. These activities offer concrete evidence of your capabilities and kindness, helping to counteract the often unfounded negative beliefs that can come with low self-esteem or anxious attachment.

Practical exercises tailored to boost self-esteem are invaluable tools in this journey. One such exercise is the 'self-appreciation diary', where you set aside a few minutes each day to jot down things you appreciate about yourself—qualities you're proud of or actions you've taken that reflect your values. This practice can gradually shift your focus from what you feel you lack to what you inherently possess. Another powerful exercise is 'assertiveness training', where you learn to express your needs and boundaries clearly and respectfully. For someone with an anxious attachment style, being able to state your needs assertively can be incredibly empowering. It reduces the tendency to engage in people-pleasing behaviors, which often come at the expense of your own well-being, thereby enhancing self-esteem.

The positive impact of improved self-esteem on modifying anxious attachment behaviors is profound. As your self-esteem grows, you'll likely notice a decrease in the intensity of your attachment anxieties. Relationships will no longer feel like tests that you must pass to prove your worth; instead, they become opportunities to connect and share, with less fear of rejection or abandonment clouding your interactions. You'll respond to relationship challenges with more resilience and less panic. This improves your relationship satisfaction and contributes to a more balanced emotional life, where your happiness is not excessively dependent on how others perceive or treat you.

In essence, cultivating strong self-esteem is crucial in mitigating the effects of anxious attachment. It provides a more stable emotional foundation, reducing the neediness and fears that often characterize this attachment style. Instead of being a source of anxiety, relationships become a source of strength and joy, reflecting a new, healthier approach to connecting with others. As you continue to build your self-esteem, remember that each step taken is a step toward more secure attachments and a more fulfilling life.

2.6 Attachment Styles in the Digital Age: Texting, Social Media, and Dating Apps

In our hyper-connected world, where interactions can be as fleeting as a swipe or a like, understanding how digital communication impacts our attachment styles is crucial. For those with anxious attachment, the realm of texting, social media, and dating apps presents a particularly challenging landscape. These platforms, while designed to connect us, often amplify anxieties, playing on the insecurities that come with anxious attachment. Text messaging, for instance, can be a minefield. The immediate nature of texting could escalate the need for quick responses—and any delay can spiral into anxiety and misinterpretation, making you wonder about the other person's feelings or intentions.

Social media adds another layer of complexity. It's a space where life is often presented not as it is, but as people wish it to appear. For someone with anxious attachment, this can translate into constant comparisons and over-analyzing why someone didn't react to a post or story—did they not like it, or worse, are they losing interest? Similarly, dating apps, which often emphasize abundance and quick interactions, can feel overwhelming, making it challenging to form meaningful connections. The transient nature of these interactions can exacerbate feelings of insecurity and worthlessness, especially when connections fizzle out or don't progress beyond the digital realm.

Despite these challenges, the digital world also offers unique opportunities. It allows for connections that might not have been possible otherwise due to geographical distance or social anxiety. The key is learning how to manage these tools, so they serve your needs without exacerbating your anxieties. One effective strategy is setting clear boundaries around digital communication. This might mean not checking social media first thing in the morning or before bed, limiting exposure to potential stressors. In terms of dating, it could involve setting a rule for yourself about how long to chat with someone online before meeting in person, which can help prevent the build-up of unrealistic expectations and anxiety.

Another valuable approach is regular digital detoxes. These periods of disconnection from digital devices help reduce reliance on external validation, which is often sought through immediate but shallow interactions on social media and texting. A detox can also help you reconnect with yourself and your direct environment, providing a clearer perspective on what truly matters in your relationships. Practically, this might look like designing one day a week where you stay off social media and dating apps, using the time instead to engage in activities promoting self-reflection and real-world interaction.

Navigating the digital landscape with an anxious attachment style isn't about withdrawal or avoidance; it's about creating a balanced approach that honors your need for connection without feeding into your anxieties. By implementing these strategies, you can start using digital tools in a way that supports your journey toward secure attachment rather than detracting from it.

As this chapter wraps up, we've explored how the pervasive influence of digital communication can significantly impact those with anxious attachment, often turning minor interactions into sources of significant stress. However, by adopting mindful usage practices and setting boundaries, it's possible to mitigate these effects and harness these powerful tools for positive personal connections. These insights deepen your understanding of how attachment styles play out in modern contexts and equip you with practical tools to navigate these dynamics more effectively. As we move forward, the focus will shift from understanding and managing external influences to fostering internal strength and resilience, essential for anyone looking to transform their approach to relationships and attachment.

The Psychology Behind Anxious Attachment

I magine sitting in a quaint coffee shop, nestled in a bustling city. Through the steam rising from your cup, you observe patrons entering and exiting. Each person's approach to the heavy, wooden door reveals a glimpse into their inner world—a world shaped by their experiences, fears, and hopes.

A young woman hesitates at the door, glancing nervously at her phone, seeking reassurance that never arrives. Tentatively, she pushes the door open, mirroring her cautious approach to relationships—a minefield of potential rejection.

A middle-aged man strides confidently towards the entrance, briefcase in hand. His movements are purposeful, opening the door effortlessly. He navigates life's challenges with self-assuredness, reflecting secure attachments from supportive relationships.

Two friends approach together, chatting excitedly. Their laughter echoes as they playfully jostle to be first through the door. Their bond demonstrates mutual trust—a comfort of secure attachments, where they can be themselves.

A solitary figure lingers, his hand hesitating on the handle. His furrowed brow reveals inner turmoil, uncertain whether to enter or retreat—a struggle mirroring the challenges of anxious attachment.

Attachment theory helps us understand the mechanisms behind our relational dynamics, much like watching those approaches to an uncomplicated door. This chapter delves into the foundational work of John Bowlby, the evolution of his theories, and their significant impact on our adult relationships, offering a contemporary perspective on how these theories operate in today's intricate social landscape.

3.1 Bowlby's Theory Revisited: Modern Interpretations

Foundations of Attachment Theory

Attachment theory, developed by John Bowlby, explains how early caregiver relationships shape adult connections. Anxious attachment stems from inconsistent caregiving, leading to hypersensitivity to rejection and abandonment cues. This theory highlights the lasting impact of early emotional bonds on adult relationship dynamics. Be mindful that critics note Bowlby's theory may overemphasize childhood influence, neglecting later life experiences. Cultural adaptations highlight varying independence norms, expanding the theory's global relevance across diverse relationships.

Since Bowlby's time, our grasp of attachment theory has deepened, especially regarding anxious attachment. Contemporary psychology melds Bowlby's insights with the latest in brain science, behavior studies, and emotional intelligence. Now, we understand that the brain's ability to change—its neuroplasticity—means that anxious attachment patterns can be reshaped with specific psychological strategies.

3.2 Cognitive Behavioral Perspectives on Attachment

Cognitive Behavioral Therapy (CBT) is a powerful tool for addressing attachment issues in mental health. It focuses on how our thoughts, emotions, and actions interact, aiming to break patterns of anxious attachment. By recognizing and challenging cognitive distortions—like catastrophizing or mind-reading—CBT helps individuals manage negative emotions and improve relationship dynamics.

CBT encourages monitoring thoughts, questioning their accuracy, and replacing them with more realistic alternatives. For example, instead of assuming a partner's silence means they're losing interest, consider they might be busy. Behavioral experiments are also key, where individuals test beliefs like fear of expressing needs, often finding outcomes are less negative than expected.

Reframing is another CBT technique, helping individuals see themselves and situations more positively. For instance, shifting from "I'm too needy" to "I have valid needs" improves self-esteem and fosters healthier relationships. By integrating these CBT strategies, individuals can reduce anxiety, enhance relational skills, and cultivate more secure connections in the long run.

3.3 Breaking Free from the Victim Mentality

In navigating the intricate web of human emotions and connections, individuals with an anxious attachment style may inadvertently adopt a victim mentality. This mindset is often characterized by helplessness and a belief that one is at the mercy of life's challenges and the complexities of relationships. Such a perspective can lead to viewing oneself as perpetually sidelined or wronged, passively enduring events rather than actively shaping them. This outlook not only hinders personal development but also reinforces the cycle of anxiety and insecurity that burdens relationships.

Recognizing this victim mentality in yourself can be both challenging and transformative. It often requires you to confront uncomfortable truths about how you interpret the interactions and events in your life. Signs that you might be succumbing to a victim mentality include:

- Frequently feeling powerless in relationships.
- Blaming others for your emotional state.
- A persistent belief that you have less control over your life than others do.

This mindset can lead to resignation, which prevents proactive change. It keeps you in a cycle of passivity and misses opportunities for growth and happiness.

Shifting from a victim mentality to a more empowered mindset involves acknowledging that while you cannot control every aspect of your life, you can always control your responses. This shift is crucial in overcoming anxious attachment, as it encourages you to actively shape your emotional landscape and the dynamics of your relationships. One effective strategy is to practice reframing challenges as opportunities. For example, instead of viewing a partner's need for space as a personal slight or a prelude to abandonment, you can see it as an opportunity to explore your interests or connect with friends, enriching your life and potentially bringing more balance to your relationship.

Empowerment through action is about embracing your capacity to effect change, both internally in your mindset and externally in your actions. It involves setting small, achievable goals reinforcing your agency, like expressing your needs in a relationship or setting boundaries around your time and emotional resources. Each step taken is a reaffirmation of your ability to influence your life's path, gradually helping to dismantle the ingrained patterns of thought that contribute to a victim mentality. This proactive approach shifts how you view yourself and your relational role and how you interact with others, fostering relationships based on mutual respect and personal integrity.

These steps require courage and persistence, as old habits and mind-sets are not easily shed. However, transforming from a passive recipient of life's whims to an active participant in your happiness and well-being is both possible and profoundly rewarding. Recognizing and addressing the victim mentality, shifting your perspective, and taking empowered action pave the way for a life characterized by greater confidence, healthier relationships, and an enduring sense of personal agency. Each step forward in this process diminishes the hold of anxious attachment and enhances your overall life satisfaction and emotional resilience.

As we wrap up this exploration of breaking free from the victim mentality, the journey we've embarked on in this chapter is a testament to the power of self-reflection and proactive change. By understanding the dynamics of a victim mentality and learning to step into a role of empowerment, you set the stage for more authentic and fulfilling relationships. This transformation process is a personal triumph and a relational aid, fostering deeper connections based on genuine interaction and mutual growth. As we move forward, remember that each step taken toward empowerment is a step away from the shadows of past attachments and toward a brighter, more secure relational future.

A Midway Call to Compassion

As we near the halfway point of our journey here on understanding where anxious attachment comes from, it is my hope and intention that you are receiving value and a renewed sense of confidence that anxious attachment *can* be overcome and a brighter future awaits you on the other side.

Know that you aren't alone in this journey of healing.

People who extend kindness without expecting anything in return often find profound healing and fulfillment.

So, let's seize the opportunity together.

To make that possibility a reality, I have a question for you...

Would you extend a helping hand to someone you've never met, even if your kindness went unnoticed?

Who is this person, you may wonder? They are akin to you—or at least, to who you once were. They seek guidance, yearn for transformation, and crave understanding, yet they struggle to find their way forward.

Our mission is to make the journey of overcoming anxious attachment accessible to all. Every endeavor I undertake is fueled by this mission. And, the key to fulfilling that mission lies in reaching... well...everyone.

This is where you come in. As it turns out, most individuals *do* judge a book by its cover (and its reviews). So, here's my humble request on behalf of all those who grapple with the struggles of anxious attachment:

Would you lend your voice by leaving a review for this book?

Your contribution demands no monetary investment and takes less than a minute to execute. Yet, it possesses the potential to alter the trajectory of a fellow reader's life; enabling them to:

- Trust in themselves and others with unwavering confidence
- Break free from childhood wounds toward genuine healing
- Cultivate the robust relationships they ardently desire, liberated from persistent self-doubt

Simply scan the QR code below to share your thoughts:

With heartfelt gratitude, I extend my thanks to you. Now, let's resume our journey with the techniques you can use to truly overcome anxious attachment with greater ease faster than you ever thought possible.

- Your Guide, Avery Parker

PS - Fun fact: If you provide something of value to another person, it makes you more valuable to them. If you'd like goodwill straight from another individual looking to overcome anxious attachment - and you believe this book will help them - please share the link to send them to the book as well.

Building Emotional Resilience

In a cozy café nestled among city skyscrapers, Maya found herself drawn to Ethan's warm smile and easygoing charm. They bonded over their shared love for art and travel, and soon, a budding romance bloomed between them. Yet, beneath Maya's confident exterior in her career, she wrestled with deep-seated fears of being abandoned, rooted in past relationships that had left her feeling unworthy.

One crisp autumn afternoon, as they sipped lattes in their favorite corner of the café, Maya couldn't shake her anxieties any longer. She stared into her cup, the swirl of steam mirroring her swirling thoughts. Finally, she took a deep breath and turned to Ethan, her voice hesitant but determined.

"Ethan, can I share something with you?" Maya began, her fingers nervously tracing the rim of her mug. "I sometimes worry that I'm not enough for you, that maybe I'm too much."

Ethan's gaze softened, his hand reaching across the table to gently cover Maya's trembling fingers. "Maya, I care deeply about you," he said sincerely. "I want us to build something meaningful together, and that starts with trust and honesty."

Maya felt a rush of relief and vulnerability as Ethan's reassuring words opened a door to a deeper connection. Maya began journaling her thoughts, challenging negative stories, and relying on Ethan's support. Their bond strengthened through shared moments, navigating life's challenges with newfound resilience. In the café, Maya realized resilience in relationships meant embracing fears with courage, choosing love over fear, one heartfelt gesture at a time.

Resilience is often pictured as the grand ability to bounce back from massive setbacks or traumas. However, as we can see from Maya's story, true resilience, especially in relationships and emotional health, is more about the subtle, daily acts of courage and perseverance. It's about the strength to face your fears of abandonment, to remain present despite inner turmoil, and to consistently align your actions with your needs and values, even when anxiety tries to steer you off course. Building emotional resilience is particularly crucial if you grapple with anxious attachment, as it arms you with tools to navigate the emotional highs and lows, helping you forge healthier, more stable relationships.

4.1 The Art of Self-Regulation: Techniques That Work

Understanding Self-Regulation

Ever wondered how to keep your cool when emotions run high? That's self-regulation in action. It's about steering your feelings and actions towards long-term goals, rather than getting swept up in the moment. For those grappling with anxious attachment, mastering self-regulation is game-changing. Picture the difference between bombarding your partner with texts when they're busy versus giving them space while managing your own anxiety—huge, right? It's not about bottling up feelings but making smart choices that keep relationships and sanity intact. The following techniques will help you keep your self-regulation in check and in turn, help you overcome your anxious attachment..

Techniques to Help with Self Regulation

Breathing Techniques:

- Deliberate, mindful breathing exercises to calm your nervous system.
- Try the 4-4-4 breathing technique: inhale deeply through your nose for four counts, hold for one count, exhale slowly through your mouth for four counts. This activates the parasympathetic nervous system, promoting relaxation.

Emotional Grounding:

- Helps stay present during emotional upheavals.
- Use the 5-4-3-2-1 grounding technique: identify five things you see, four things you touch, three things you hear, two things you smell, and one thing you taste.
- Diverts focus from distressing emotions to the present moment. (Noor, 2002).

Routine as Regulation:

- Enhances emotional stability and predictability.
- Provides structure and comfort, reducing daily decisions and countering anxiety.
- Establish a consistent routine like morning journaling, midday walks, or nightly reading to regulate emotions throughout the day.
- By adopting these practical tools, you strengthen emotional resilience and improve your ability to handle anxious attachment, fostering a more balanced and fulfilling life

These are just a few of many techniques that can be used to help ground yourself. The following sections will explore some other options that work for many people when building emotional resilience.

4.2 Cultivating Mindfulness: A Path to Presence

Mindfulness, an ancient practice, is now a game-changer for modern mental wellness, especially for those with anxious attachment. At its heart, mindfulness means staying aware of our thoughts, feelings, bodily sensations, and surroundings with an open and curious attitude.

For those with anxious attachment, mindfulness can be a lifesaver. It helps shift focus from future worries and past regrets to the manageable present, breaking the anxiety cycle that fuels fears about relationship stability and self-worth.

Mindfulness builds mental discipline, training the brain to stay present and avoid getting lost in 'what-ifs.' For someone with anxious attachment, this means learning to observe insecurity or fear without immediately reacting. These feelings are just passing emotions, not fixed truths. Regular mindfulness practice can rewire your brain, creating new pathways of calm and stability.

Daily mindfulness doesn't have to be daunting. Simply dedicate a few minutes to focus on one task:

- Morning Coffee: As you sip your coffee, notice its aroma, the warmth of the cup, and the taste.
- Showering: Focus on the sensation of the water on your skin, the scent of your soap, and the sound of the water.
- Commuting: Pay attention to the sights around you, the sounds of the city, or the feel of the steering wheel in your hands.

This 'informal mindfulness' helps you stay present throughout the day without extra meditation time.

Mindful listening is another powerful tool, especially for improving relationship communication—a common issue for those with anxious attachment. It means fully focusing on the speaker, not planning your response or getting distracted by internal dialogue.

This practice fosters genuine understanding and connection, reducing misunderstandings and relationship anxiety:

- During Conversations: Listen without interrupting. Notice the speaker's tone and body language.
- Reflecting: Before responding, take a moment to reflect on what was said.
- Non-verbal Cues: Pay attention to non-verbal cues to understand the speaker's emotions better.

By incorporating these mindfulness practices, you manage anxious attachment symptoms at their roots. Over time, you'll likely notice less emotional turmoil, more tranquility, and a greater ability to enjoy relationships without constant anxiety. This transformation, achieved through the simple act of being present, highlights mindfulness's power to create lasting change in your life and relationships.

4.3 Emotional Agility: Navigating Feelings with Ease

What is Emotional Agility?

Emotional agility is about managing thoughts and emotions with mindfulness and intention, enabling adaptive responses. This is crucial for those with anxious attachment, who often spiral into self-doubt and counterproductive behaviors. Emotional agility helps pause between being triggered and reacting, allowing one to take actions that reflect their core values and desired selves.

Identifying and Using Emotions

The journey toward emotional agility begins with the vital yet challenging task of identifying and labeling your emotions. Emotions can intertwine and be hard to understand. Recognize emotions as data, not commands. Keep an emotion journal to document strong emotions, situations, and physical sensations.

After identifying emotions, the next step is acceptance. Accepting emotions can be challenging for those with anxious attachment. Cultivate a non-judgmental attitude toward emotions, understanding they are neither good nor bad.

Using Emotions Constructively

Finally, learning to use your emotions constructively can change how you manage anxious attachment. You can view emotions as tools for growth and relationship improvement. For instance, you can use jealousy as a cue to explore insecurities or discuss needs with your partner. Engaging in constructive conversations can turn emotional distress into opportunities for deeper understanding and enhanced intimacy.

So, emotional agility is not about controlling emotions to avoid feeling deeply but engaging with them consciously and constructively. This skill requires practice, patience, and perseverance but offers significant rewards in personal mastery and relationship satisfaction. Cultivating emotional agility helps manage anxious attachment and enjoy the dynamic landscape of human emotion and connection.

4.4 Breaking the Anxiety-Insecurity Loop

Imagine walking down a spiral staircase where each step fueled by anxiety leads you deeper into insecurity. That's the anxiety-insecurity feedback loop in anxious attachment. Anxiety about relationships pushes you to act in ways that push others away, making you feel even more insecure and anxious. Breaking this loop is key to healthier relationships.

The first step is to recognize when you're in the loop. Understand that your constant need for reassurance stems from deep fears of abandonment. Challenge this by using 'if-then' planning. For example, if you feel the urge to check in with your partner too much, take a walk or breathe deeply first. Gradually extend the time between reassurance-seeking to get comfortable with uncertainty and reduce anxiety.

Take Alex: he used 'if-then' planning to focus on hobbies, reducing his relationship anxiety and improving interactions with his partner. Jamie stretched the time between seeking reassurance and found her fears unfounded, leading to more trust and affection.

Preventing the loop starts with self-awareness and good communication. Reflect regularly to catch early signs of anxiety, and talk openly with your partner about your fears and needs to avoid misunderstandings. Set personal boundaries, like not checking work emails during family time, to maintain balance and support relationship health.

By recognizing and interrupting this loop, you can create secure, resilient relationships and transform how you connect with others, making interactions more fulfilling and fun.

4.5 From Reactivity to Responsivity: A Shift in Approach

Navigating relationships, especially with anxious attachment, requires understanding the difference between reactivity and responsivity. Reactivity is impulsive and emotion-driven, while responsiveness involves thoughtful, deliberate actions aligned with core values and relationship goals.

Some key practices for the shift include:

1. Pausing and Reflecting:

- Pause in the Moment: Before reacting, take a brief pause. This creates space to assess your emotional state.
- Self-Awareness: Recognize triggers, like a tightening chest when a text goes unanswered or anger at perceived criticism.
- Ask Questions: "Why am I feeling this? What's triggering me? Does my impulse align with how I want to handle this?"

Example: Instead of reacting with anger, take a deep breath and think: "I feel worried when I don't hear from you. Can we talk about improving our communication?"

2. Choosing Conscious Responses:

- Assess and Respond: After pausing, choose a response that benefits the relationship rather than reacting impulsively.
- Express Constructively: Communicate feelings in ways that open dialogue, not shut it down.

- Let Go of Small Triggers: Focus on what truly matters rather than minor anxieties.

Example: Instead of accusing your partner, express your feelings calmly focusing on how the behavior makes you feel without blaming the individual. For example: "I feel worried when I don't hear from you."

3. Benefits of Responsivity:

- Builds Trust: Handling emotions thoughtfully and communicating calmly builds a foundation of trust and safety.
- Enhances Interaction Quality: Turns conversations into opportunities for deeper understanding and connection.
- Reduces Anxiety: Manages anxiety more constructively, breaking the cycle of reactive behaviors.

Example: Instead of pushing your partner away, you create a space for mutual respect and understanding.

4. Personal Growth and Relationship Transformation:

- Develops Patience: Learning to pause and reflect teaches patience.
- Promotes Reflection: Regular assessment of your responses helps in aligning actions with your values.
- Fosters Balance: Cultivates a more fulfilling and balanced life, improving overall relationship satisfaction.

Example: By practicing these skills, you'll find your relationships healthier and more peaceful, and you'll be more at ease with yourself.

As we can see, transforming from reactivity to responsivity isn't just about better relationships... It's about personal growth. Embracing patience, reflection, and thoughtful action will cultivate more fulfilling relationships and better balance in your life.

4.6 The Power of Positive Self-Talk

Navigating relationships with anxious attachment can feel like a constant battle with doubts and fears. Negative self-talk can amplify these anxieties, creating cycles of self-doubt and stress. However, positive self-talk can shift this dynamic, fostering self-assurance and healthier relationship patterns.

Try starting your day with thoughts like, "I deserve love and respect," instead of doubting your worth. Positive self-talk sets a tone of self-acceptance, transforming interactions and reducing anxiety. By doing this, you are reframing your thoughts and using cognitive behavioral techniques to change negative thought patterns.

For example, instead of thinking, "My partner is late because they don't care about me," reframe it to, "My partner is late; they must be held up. I know we both value our time together." This approach offers a balanced perspective, reducing unnecessary anguish and fostering understanding.

Affirmations are a great way for us to reshape subconscious beliefs. When repeated often, these positive, empowering statements can help reshape your subconscious beliefs about yourself and your relationships.

Here are some examples:

- "I am deserving of a secure, loving relationship."
- "I trust in my worth and my partner's commitment."

You can integrate affirmations like this into your daily routine by saying them each morning, writing them in your journal, or posting them where you'll see them. This approach mitigates attachment-related anxieties and builds a positive, resilient self-identity, leading to more fulfilling and less fear-driven relationships.

Navigating anxious attachment calls for a reliable self-care routine that boosts resilience and nurtures well-being amid life's hustle and bustle. It's not just about pampering, it's about staying grounded and reducing the need for constant validation, creating healthier relationship dynamics.

It's crucial that you develop a personalized approach to self-care tailored to your needs. But, how do you know what you need? Start by reflecting on activities that recharge you, whether it's reading, yoga, or painting. Then, choose activities that bring intrinsic joy rather than feeling like chores. Even ten minutes daily of your chosen activity can significantly enhance emotional equilibrium. Activities like music, gardening, or baking shift focus from worries to present joys. But, it's important to focus on the pleasure of the activity itself, not on performance or outcomes.

Here is an example of a positive self-care routine:

- Morning Meditation: Start the day with 10 minutes of guided meditation to center your mind.
- Journaling: Reflect on your thoughts and emotions for clarity and self-awareness.

- Physical Activity: Engage in 30 minutes of yoga or a brisk walk to energize your body.
- Creative Outlet: Spend 20 minutes painting or playing a musical instrument to unwind.
- Healthy Nutrition: Prepare and enjoy a balanced meal that nourishes your body and mind.
- Digital Detox: Disconnect from screens an hour before bed to improve sleep quality.
- Nightly Relaxation: Wind down with a soothing bath or reading a book to relax your mind.

You can customize these activities based on what brings you joy and relaxation, ensuring your routine supports your emotional and mental well-being. Once you have this routine, you need to set boundaries and communicate clearly with others about its importance for your well-being. Doing so is not selfish; it's a commitment to your mental and emotional health. By making self-care a daily priority, you empower yourself to manage anxious attachment effectively and model emotional health for others. This commitment fosters resilience, joy, and healthier relationships, creating a lasting sense of well-being in all aspects of life.

Healing from Within

As the sun dipped below the horizon, casting a golden hue over the tranquil garden, Elena wandered along the winding paths, her mind racing with thoughts. She had recently started exploring the concept of healing her inner child and was eager to discuss it with someone who might understand. She spotted a bench near a bubbling fountain and decided to sit down, her fingers lightly tracing the edges of a book she had brought along.

Moments later, she noticed a familiar figure approaching. It was Jake, a friend she had met at a local meditation class. He seemed lost in his own thoughts but smiled warmly when he saw her.

"Hey, Elena," Jake greeted, taking a seat beside her. "What brings you here this evening?"

Elena sighed, glancing at the book in her lap. "I've been reading about reconnecting with your inner child. It's been quite enlightening, but also a bit overwhelming. I needed some fresh air to process it all."

Jake nodded, his expression turning thoughtful. "That's a powerful topic. I've been diving into something similar lately. How past traumas shape our present attachments. It's incredible how much of our adult behavior is rooted in childhood experiences."

Elena's eyes lit up. "Exactly! I was just reading about that. How trauma, especially in early years, can lead to anxious attachment patterns. For example, I grew up with a father who was constantly unreliable. Now I can see how it taught me to distrust others and to rely solely on myself."

Jake listened intently. "I can relate to that. My childhood was marked by neglect and emotional abuse. It left me with a constant fear of rejection and abandonment in my adult relationships. It's like these survival strategies we developed as kids are still influencing us now."

Elena nodded in agreement. "Yes, these reactions aren't irrational. They're survival strategies we developed in response to unpredictable environments. But it's time we start healing those wounds. Have you tried any exercises to connect with your inner child?"

Jake leaned back, his gaze fixed on the sky. "I've started some journaling and meditation. Creating a safe space to connect with my younger self. Asking questions like, 'What do you need?' and 'What fears do you hold?' It's been quite revealing."

Elena smiled. "That's wonderful. I've found that initiating a dialogue with my inner child helps a lot. Visualizing a safe place where I can meet my younger self, offering words of comfort and reassurance. It's a deeply emotional process, but so necessary."

Jake's eyes softened. "It sounds like you're making real progress. Integrating the inner child means acknowledging their fears and needs without letting them define you. Embracing childhood traits like curiosity and resilience while also using adult skills like boundary setting and self-care. It's a balance that can foster mature, secure relationships."

Elena took a deep breath. "And then there's the aspect of forgiveness. Forgiving ourselves and others. It's so crucial for overcoming anxious attachment. It's not about condoning past actions but freeing ourselves from their emotional hold."

Jake nodded. "Self-forgiveness is tough but essential. Recognizing past actions as growth opportunities rather than judgments of our worth. Writing a forgiveness letter to myself has helped release some of the inner resentment and nurtured self-compassion."

Elena added, "And forgiving those who contributed to our anxious attachment. It's about freeing ourselves from their emotional grip. Empathy can help us understand their perspective, making forgiveness easier."

Jake sighed contentedly. "The journey of self-healing is fragile yet transformative. Every step heals past traumas and strengthens us for a future characterized by secure, understanding, and deeply connected relationships. Engaging in heartfelt dialogues with our inner child and offering moments of reassurance and understanding can lay the groundwork for evolving into adults who can love deeply and fearlessly."

Elena smiled, feeling a sense of solidarity. "And then there's discovering our true needs. Reflecting daily to uncover what truly brings us joy and contentment. Asking ourselves, 'What do I need more or less of in my life right now?' This reflection lays the foundation for understanding our needs authentically."

Jake agreed. "Effective communication of these needs is key. Using 'I' statements to express ourselves directly fosters openness and understanding. Aligning our actions with identified needs ensures authenticity in daily life."

Elena gazed at the fountain, feeling a wave of calm wash over her. "And embracing vulnerability. It's seen as a weakness, but it's actually a courageous act of opening up to being fully known, risks included. For those with anxious attachment, where fear of rejection looms large, redefining vulnerability as strength can transform relationship dynamics."

Jake's eyes met hers. "Vulnerability fosters authenticity and strengthens emotional bonds. Starting with small, low-risk expressions of vulnerability builds confidence and encourages deeper connections based on honesty and openness."

Elena nodded. "Overcoming the fear of vulnerability involves challenging negative thoughts and reframing them to focus on the potential for deeper connections rather than rejection. Gradual exposure to vulnerable situations reinforces resilience and reduces fear over time."

Jake smiled. "Ultimately, embracing vulnerability unlocks richer, more fulfilling relationships based on mutual understanding and respect. Each step forward enriches connections and strengthens our self-perception. True strength lies in the courage to be seen and loved for who we truly are."

As the sun set, casting a warm glow over the garden, Elena and Jake continued their conversation, delving deeper into their personal journeys of healing and self-discovery. They found comfort in knowing they were not alone, and that each step they took towards understanding and nurturing their inner child brought them closer to a future filled with secure, loving relationships.

———

This chapter invites you to explore one of the most poignant paths: reconnecting with your inner child. The roots of our present anxieties and attachment styles are often buried deep in our childhood experiences. We can address these roots by nurturing and healing our inner child, profoundly transforming our adult relationships and attachment styles.

5.1 How Past Traumas Shape Present Attachments

Trauma can cast long shadows over our current relationships, subtly coloring how we perceive and interact with others. It is like wearing sunglasses indoors… it affects everything! When we experience things like neglect or emotional ups and downs early on, it can leave us with anxious attachment patterns that stick around into adulthood.

As I mentioned before, in my own life, growing up with a father who repeatedly let me down taught me early on to distrust others and made me think I had to rely solely on myself.

These reactions aren't just quirks.. they're survival skills created in response to unpredictable environments. And believe me, those childhood lessons played a big part in how I handled trust and intimacy as I grew up.

5.2 Conversations with Your Inner Child: Healing Old Wounds

Understanding and Integrating the Inner Child

The inner child isn't just a metaphor but a psychological tool embodying our adult self's childhood emotions. It holds fears, joys, traumas, and hopes, shaping how we relate today. For those with anxious attachment, the inner child feels vulnerable, carrying unprocessed emotional scars from neglect or inconsistency. Recognizing and nurturing this part of us is crucial for understanding and healing patterns of fear and insecurity in relationships.

Initiate a dialogue through journaling or meditation. Create a safe space to connect with your younger self. Ask questions like, "What do you need?" or "What fears do you hold?" Listen without judgment, offering compassion and reassurance. This process deepens understanding and resolves emotional patterns influencing your present self.

Integrating your inner child acknowledges their fears and needs without defining you. Embrace childhood traits like curiosity and resilience alongside adult skills like boundary setting and self-care. This balance fosters mature, secure relationships with enhanced emotional intelligence.

Inner Child Healing Exercise

Healing our inner child is like discovering buried treasure within ourselves—it takes patience and a whole lot of compassion. This exercise is all about reconnecting with that vulnerable part of us that holds onto childhood emotions, fears, joys, traumas, and dreams. By giving our inner child the attention and care they deserve, we can start to mend old wounds, understand our attachment styles better, and build healthier relationships.

To facilitate a deeper connection with your inner child, consider this visual exercise:

1. Find a quiet space where you won't be disturbed.
2. Close your eyes and take several deep breaths, grounding yourself in the present.
3. Visualize a safe, peaceful place. Imagine your inner child there. See them clearly—what are they doing? How do they look?
4. Approach them with openness and compassion. Ask them what they need from you right now.
5. Listen to their response. Offer them words of comfort, understanding, or encouragement.
6. Imagine embracing them, letting them know they are safe and loved.
7. Take a few moments to feel the emotional connection and reassurance you've provided.
8. When you're ready, gently bring yourself back to the present.

Make this exercise a regular practice to strengthen your bond with your inner child. This nurturing process can lead to profound healing and integration, transforming the way you approach relationships and attachment.

As you navigate this journey of self-healing through nurturing your inner child, remember each step is a powerful stride toward healing past wounds and preparing yourself for relationships filled with security, understanding, and deep connection. Engaging in heartfelt conversations with your inner child, offering moments of reassurance and empathy, lays the groundwork for embracing love that is profound, liberating, and fearless.

5.3 Forgiving Yourself and Others: Letting Go of the Past

Forgiveness, whispered in healing circles, is key to conquering anxious attachment. It means letting go of past grievances, freeing yourself and others from resentment and pain. It's a vital step toward emotional freedom and healthier connections. Embracing forgiveness quenches emotional fires, paving the way for new, healthier relationships based on the present, not the past.

Self-forgiveness is tough but essential in overcoming anxious attachment. It's about showing yourself the same compassion you'd give a friend, recognizing past actions as growth opportunities, not judgments of your worth. Writing a forgiveness letter to yourself can release inner resentment and nurture self-compassion.

Forgiving others who contributed to anxious attachment is crucial too. It's not about condoning actions but freeing yourself from their emotional hold. Empathy helps us understand their perspective, easing the path to forgiveness.

The power of forgiveness lies in moving forward. It liberates from past hurts, fostering open, peaceful interactions. This shift transforms relationships into secure, fulfilling connections based on mutual respect and present realities.

Engaging in forgiveness sparks profound transformations, reshaping how you view the past and navigate present relationships. It's a journey toward a more secure, confident, and connected self—

capable of giving and receiving love free from the shadows of the past holding you back.

5.4 The Journey of Self-Discovery: Uncovering Your True Needs

Knowing your own needs is like mastering the recipe for a perfect dish... you've got to understand your ingredients! This is especially crucial for those dealing with anxious attachment, who often put others' needs ahead of their own.

Start by checking in with yourself daily to uncover what really lights you up. Ask deep questions like, "What's missing or overwhelming in my life right now?" This introspection sets the stage for getting to know your needs on a deeper level.

Next, you may want to try an exercise like a 'Needs Inventory.' List out your emotional, physical, intellectual, and spiritual needs, ranking them by how important they are to your well-being. This helps guide decisions and set boundaries that honor your true self.

When it comes to sharing these needs, pick calm moments to speak your truth using "I" statements; this way of communicating your needs and experiences beginning with "I" followed by a description of your emotions or perceptions fosters openness and mutual understanding in your relationships. For example, you might say "I feel frustrated when I get interrupted" rather than saying "You always interrupt me."

Make sure your actions line up with those identified needs to live authentically day-to-day. Adjust your priorities as necessary to stay fulfilled and in control, crafting a life that truly resonates with who you are.

Embrace this journey of self-discovery as steps toward a more empowered and genuine existence. Let your relationships and personal choices reflect the real you, bringing completeness and joy to every corner of your life.

5.5 Embracing Vulnerability: Strength in Being Open

Vulnerability, often mistaken for weakness, is actually a brave act of opening up fully, despite the risks. For those grappling with anxious attachment and the looming fear of rejection, reframing vulnerability as a strength can revolutionize relationship dynamics, nurturing deeper connections and genuine self-expression.

By embracing vulnerability, we foster authenticity and fortify emotional bonds, demonstrating trust and value in our relationships. Starting with small, low-risk displays of vulnerability builds confidence and encourages more profound connections built on honesty and openness.

Overcoming the fear of vulnerability means challenging negative thoughts and reshaping them to focus on the potential for deeper connections rather than the fear of rejection. Gradually exposing ourselves to vulnerable situations strengthens resilience and diminishes fear over time.

Ultimately, embracing vulnerability unlocks richer, more fulfilling relationships founded on mutual understanding and respect. Each step forward enriches connections and bolsters self-perception, proving that real strength lies in the courage to be authentically seen and loved for who we truly are.

Practical Tools for Everyday Life

On a bright Saturday morning, Ava and Liam met at their favorite coffee shop near the city park. The shop, with its cozy ambiance and aroma of freshly brewed coffee, was a sanctuary where they often retreated to escape their busy lives and engage in meaningful conversations.

As they settled into their seats, Ava took a deep breath, savoring the tranquility. "Liam, I've been thinking a lot about our last conversation on attachment styles and healing from past traumas. It's amazing how our childhood experiences shape us."

Liam nodded, taking a sip of his cappuccino. "Absolutely, Ava. I've been reading more about setting boundaries and communicating needs effectively. It's been a game-changer for me."

"That sounds interesting. I've always struggled with expressing my needs without feeling guilty or afraid of rejection. How do you manage to do it?" Ava asked.

Liam answered, ""It's a process, but clarity is key. You need to be clear on what you truly need and why it matters. For instance, if you need time alone to recharge, express it clearly: 'I need some quiet time each day to relax and gather my thoughts.'"

"I can see how that would help. I often find myself agreeing to things I don't want to do just to avoid conflict."

Liam nodded. "That's where assertiveness comes in. It's about confidently and honestly expressing your needs while respecting others. Practice using 'I' statements and open body language. It helps to role-play scenarios to build confidence."

Ava leaned back, pondering Liam's advice. "Role-playing sounds useful. I guess it's also important to handle rejection better."

"Definitely. Fear of rejection can be a huge barrier. Try to see rejection as a sign of misaligned needs, not a personal failure. Always remember you are worthy just as you are, independent of whatever others opinions may be."

They both paused, absorbing the serenity of the coffee shop, the soft murmur of conversations around them, and the occasional clatter of cups.

"I've also been thinking about conflict resolution," Ava said. "I tend to avoid conflicts, but I know that's not healthy."

Liam sighed. "Avoidance doesn't solve anything. Try de-escalation techniques. Use a 'soft startup' to express your feelings gently, like saying, 'I feel overwhelmed when our plans change at the last minute. Can we plan ahead to avoid this?' Also, use 'repair attempts' to restart conversations if they start to escalate."

"I'll give that a try. It sounds more constructive than my usual approach."

Liam smiled, feeling the warmth of their mutual understanding. "Another thing that's been transformative is practicing gratitude. It shifts focus from anxieties to appreciation, which enriches emotional well-being and improves relationships."

"I've heard of gratitude journals. Do they really make a difference?"

"Absolutely. Gratitude helps you recognize and appreciate positive actions, promoting reciprocal warmth and strengthening emotional bonds. It's like a warm light that softens life's sharper edges."

Ava's face lit up with a newfound determination. "I'm going to start a gratitude journal and practice these tips. It's time I take control of my emotional and relational health!"

Liam: "That's the spirit! Remember, it's all about integrating these tools into your daily life. Set boundaries, communicate needs effectively, navigate conflicts with confidence, and embrace gratitude. It's a journey, but it's worth it."

Walking out of the coffee shop, they felt ready to face the world, knowing they had the tools to manage their emotional and mental traffic effectively. The city's bustle seemed less daunting, each street a new opportunity to apply what they had learned, enhancing their well-being and the health of their relationships.

6.1 Practical Tips for Communicating Needs Without Fear

In the rhythm of daily life, expressing your needs clearly is not just beneficial—it's essential for nurturing personal happiness and fostering healthy relationships. Effective communication acts as a bridge between your inner desires and the external world of social interactions, ensuring your voice is heard while respecting others.

Key Strategies:

- **Clarity is Key:** Start by gaining clarity on what you truly need and why it matters to you. Identify non-negotiables versus areas where flexibility is possible. For instance, if quality time is crucial for you, express it clearly: "I feel loved and connected when we have uninterrupted time together. Could we schedule date nights weekly on Thursdays?"
- **Assertiveness Empowers:** Assertiveness isn't about being pushy; it's about confidently and honestly expressing your needs while respecting others. Practice stating your needs using "I" statements and maintaining open body language. Role-play scenarios to build confidence in handling real-life situations.
- **Resilience Against Rejection:** Fear of rejection can inhibit expressing needs. Change your perspective: rejection often signifies misaligned needs, not personal failure. Strengthen self-worth independently of others' opinions through self-affirmation and supportive relationships.

Mastering these skills fosters an environment where needs are openly and respectfully addressed. This approach cultivates deeper connections and more harmonious interactions in your relationships. As you integrate these strategies, observe positive shifts in communication dynamics, reaffirming the transformative power of expressing needs confidently and without fear. By implementing these practical tools, you empower yourself to navigate relationships with clarity, assertiveness, and empathy, laying the groundwork for fulfilling and mutually respectful interactions.

6.2 Navigating Conflict with Confidence

In any relationship, conflict is like the wild waves in an ocean... totally natural and sometimes exhilarating. It's not a sign to panic but a chance for partners to dive deeper, understand each other better, and grow together. By seeing conflict as an opportunity to strengthen your bond, you can totally transform how you approach challenges and emerge stronger.

Key Strategies:

- **Mindset Shift:** View conflict as an opportunity rather than a battle. This shift opens doors to greater insight into each other's desires, fears, and values, promoting a collaborative approach to resolving differences.
- **De-escalation Techniques:** Maintain composure with a "soft startup," where you express your feelings and needs gently. For example, say, "I feel neglected when I talk and need to feel heard," instead of accusatory statements. Utilize "repair attempts" like restarting conversations to prevent escalation.
- **Problem-Solving Together:** Approach conflicts as a mutual challenge rather than a confrontation. Define the issue objectively, brainstorm solutions together, and respect each other's viewpoints to find compromises that address both partners' needs.
- **Learning and Growth:** Reflect on each conflict to understand communication styles, triggers, and expectations better. Discuss what worked well and how to improve for future disagreements. Implementing skills like psychological self-soothing and compromise enhances conflict management.

By embracing conflict as an opportunity for improvement using strategies like calming things down, solving problems together, and learning from each conflict, you'll build a relationship that's not just strong, but more fulfilling as you build greater understanding. So, stay steady working through those challenges and watch your bond grow even tighter, setting the stage for a love that lasts.

6.3 The Role of Gratitude in Transforming Relationships

Gratitude, often likened to a warm light that softens life's sharper edges, holds profound transformative power in enhancing individual well-being and nurturing relationship health. By integrating regular gratitude practices into your life, you can cultivate resilience against daily stresses and amplify the joy found in meaningful interactions.

Some of the main benefits of Gratitude include:

- **Enhanced Emotional Wellness:** Gratitude shifts focus from anxieties to appreciation, fostering a mindset that values the contributions and kindness of others, thereby enriching emotional well-being.
- **Improved Relationship Dynamics:** Practicing gratitude helps you recognize and appreciate the positive actions of others, promoting reciprocal warmth and strengthening emotional bonds, crucial in maintaining healthy relationships.
- **Stress Reduction and Physical Health:** Research indicates that gratitude can lower stress levels, improve sleep quality, and contribute to overall physical health, enhancing your capacity to engage positively in relationships.

By integrating gratitude into your daily routine and relationship practices, you not only enhance your personal well-being but also nurture a foundation of appreciation and connection. Embrace gratitude as a powerful tool to enrich your life and watch your relationships grow deeper and more fulfilling.

In relationships, the depth and quality of connections profoundly influence our personal experiences. Moving beyond superficial interactions to cultivate meaningful bonds requires intention, understanding, and dedicated practice. It's about fostering moments that deepen mutual understanding and emotional connectivity, nurturing relationships to flourish in truly fulfilling ways.

Try some of the following Strategies for Deepening Relationships:

- **Creating Shared Experiences:** Actively engage in activities together, whether exploring new hobbies, embarking on adventures, or participating in community projects. These shared experiences build a sense of partnership, creating memorable moments and forging a unique bond through shared victories and challenges. They reveal new dimensions of each other's personalities and strengthen the connection beyond mere acquaintance.
- **Active Listening:** Practice attentive listening by focusing entirely on what the speaker is conveying, not just the words but also the underlying emotions and intentions. Show engagement through non-verbal cues like nodding and verbal affirmations such as "I understand." Reflect on what you've heard and ask clarifying questions to demonstrate genuine interest and understanding. This level of attentiveness communicates value and enhances the depth of your interactions.

- **Cultivating Empathy:** Empathy is essential for bridging emotional gaps and understanding diverse perspectives. It involves empathizing with another's feelings and experiences without judgment. Develop empathy by asking open-ended questions that encourage deeper sharing and actively listening to connect with the emotions expressed. Cultivating empathy enriches your relationships and expands your emotional horizons, fostering deeper connections based on mutual understanding and respect.

Deep connections support individual well-being by providing emotional support, understanding, and a sense of belonging within relationships. By integrating these strategies into your interactions, you nurture relationships that are resilient and nurturing, capable of withstanding challenges and evolving over time.

Cultivating Secure Attachments in Relationships

"Hey, remember when we used to argue about who gets the last slice of pizza?" Sarah chuckled as she adjusted the guitar strings. "It's like tuning an instrument, right? We've learned to listen to each other's needs instead of just clashing over toppings."

"Absolutely," Mark replied, plucking a string to test its tension. "It's about finding that sweet spot where we're both in sync, where our conversations flow like a perfect chord progression."

Sarah nodded thoughtfully. "And when we do hit that harmony, it feels like we're not just talking but really understanding each other."

Mark smiled, tuning another string delicately. "Exactly! It's about fine-tuning our communication so we can resonate with that deep emotional connection every time."

Sarah strummed a chord experimentally. "And that's what makes our relationship feel so secure and fulfilling… like we're playing the same song, together."

Thinking of this story, you will understand how fine-tuning an instrument can be used as a metaphor. Each guitar string represents a communication thread in your relationships. Just as a well-tuned instrument can resonate with beautiful harmony, a relationship grounded in secure attachment resonates with emotional depth and harmony. This chapter delves into the subtle yet profound ways you can fine-tune your interactions to cultivate a secure attachment style, transforming the quality of your connections and enriching your relational world.

7.1 Understanding the Language of Secure Attachment

Defining Secure Language

Secure attachment speaks a language of its own, characterized by verbal and non-verbal cues that foster a profound sense of safety and understanding. Words that affirm, gestures that comfort and actions that reassure are the lexicon of this language. Saying things like "I've got your back" or "I totally get where you're coming from" can work wonders, easing fears and boosting feelings of worthiness. Meanwhile, a well-timed nod, a gentle touch, or a heartfelt smile speak volumes without uttering a word. This language, rich in empathy and affirmation, forms the bedrock of relationships where each person feels cherished, seen, and secure.

Communication Techniques

Effective communication is like mastering a secret code to closeness. It's about choosing words wisely and tuning into the emotions behind them. Take mirroring, for example—repeating or paraphrasing what your partner says shows you're really tuned in, validating their feelings and deepening your connection. And don't forget inclusive language! Saying things like "Let's tackle this together" or "We've got this" builds a team spirit, tackling challenges side by side and making your bond even stronger.

Active Listening

Active listening is a dynamic and integral part of fostering security in any relationship. Think of it as the ultimate relationship power move. It's not just about hearing words; it's about getting the whole picture—emotions and all. It goes beyond hearing words to engaging with and understanding your partner's complete message. This means listening for the content and the emotions behind the words. By doing so, you can respond more accurately to your partner's needs, alleviating misunderstandings and preemptively addressing potential conflicts. Active listening involves giving undivided attention, refraining from interrupting, and reflecting back on what you've heard to confirm understanding. This practice makes your partner feel valued and heard and deepens your understanding of each other, enhancing emotional intimacy.

Positive Reinforcement

Positive reinforcement is like sprinkling magic dust on your relationship. It's all about celebrating your partner's awesome moves and qualities, which encourages more of those behaviors and creates a beautiful cycle of love and support. Whether it's thanking them for planning a killer date night or just appreciating their everyday efforts, those little shout-outs build a foundation of respect and admiration that's rock-solid.

By mastering this language of secure attachment and putting these tricks into action, you're not just leveling up your relationships... you're boosting your own happiness, too. Watch how these tools transform your interactions, making your connections deeper, more satisfying, and finely tuned to every emotional nuance.

7.2 Strategies for Building Trust: A New Foundation

Trust in a relationship is like the roots of a plant—essential yet often unseen, grounding and nourishing the connection. Without it, relationships can struggle to weather life's storms, vulnerable to even the smallest challenges. Recognizing this foundational role of trust is crucial, especially when rebuilding connections after they've been shaken.Whether eroded through small misunderstandings or shattered by significant betrayals, the restoration of trust is both a challenging and critical process. It begins with a commitment to growth and an understanding that rebuilding trust is a gradual process that involves consistent effort and patience from all parties involved.

The first step in laying a new foundation of trust involves a commitment to consistency and reliability. These are the building blocks of trust, as they provide a predictable and safe environment where both partners can feel secure. Consistency in relationships translates into actions aligning with words; it means that promises made are promises kept. When you say you will call, you do. When you agree to make changes in behaviors that hurt your partner, those changes become visible through your actions. This reliability in small, everyday actions builds a track record that gradually restores trust. It's akin to placing bricks one at a time to construct a sturdy wall. Each consistent action is a brick, contributing to the rebuilding of the relationship.

Transparency and honesty are equally critical in this rebuilding phase. They involve a willingness to openly share thoughts and feelings, even those that might be uncomfortable or difficult. Transparency means not having hidden agendas or keeping secrets that could later undermine the relationship. It requires a level of vulnerability that can be challenging, especially in a relationship recovering from mistrust. However, this openness fosters a deeper understanding and connection, allowing both partners to see and understand each other's perspectives and vulnerabilities truly. Honesty is crucial, even when it involves admitting mistakes or sharing painful truths. It signals to your partner that you value the relationship more than your comfort or fear of conflict. This kind of honesty can significantly strengthen the bonds of trust, reassuring your partner that you are committed to transparency and integrity.

Rebuilding trust after betrayal is perhaps one of the most challenging conflicts that can happen in a relationship. It requires immense emotional resilience and a strong commitment to mutual growth. The process often starts with expressing genuine remorse and an apology acknowledging the pain caused. This apology needs to be heartfelt and specific, addressing the actions that broke the trust and their emotional impact on your partner. Following this, both partners need to engage in a frank discussion about the underlying issues that led to the betrayal. This discussion should aim not only to understand 'what' happened but 'why' it happened, exploring the dynamics and personal failings that contributed to the situation. Importantly, rebuilding trust requires a plan for change that involves both partners. This plan should include practical steps and behaviors that need to be changed to avoid future betrayals. It might also involve setting new boundaries or rules for the relationship that both partners agree to adhere to.

Throughout this process, forgiveness plays a pivotal role. It does not imply forgetting or excusing the hurt caused but rather letting go of this pain's hold on your relationship. Forgiveness can be challenging and requires time and empathy from both partners. It involves seeing the situation from the other's perspective and recognizing the human imperfections that led to the mistakes. Mutual commitment to growth is essential here—both partners must be committed to learning from the past and growing together, turning a painful experience into a stepping stone for a stronger, more secure relationship. As trust is gradually restored, it's essential to acknowledge and celebrate this progress, reinforcing the positive changes and deepening the commitment to a shared future.

7.3 Balancing Independence and Intimacy in Relationships

Finding the right balance between independence and intimacy in relationships is like mastering a dance routine—too much independence, and you risk stepping out of sync; too much closeness, and you might trip over each other. It's all about finding that sweet spot where you feel free to be yourself while also deeply connected.

What if you're both dancing solo, doing your own moves, but somehow they harmonize perfectly together? You're cheering each other on, celebrating your unique quirks and passions, all while holding hands and swaying to the same rhythm.

Striking this balance is crucial, not only for the health of the relationship but for personal well-being. Maintaining independence while fostering intimacy means embracing the idea that you can be your own person, with unique desires and pursuits, while being deeply connected and committed to one another. It's about nurturing a relationship where both partners feel supported yet free to explore their individuality.

Setting and respecting healthy boundaries is foundational in achieving this balance. It is like drawing lines on the dance floor. It's not about restricting each other but ensuring you both have space to shine. You might declare certain hours for your hobbies or self-care, saying, "Hey, these evenings are my time for yoga and reading." It's about communicating what you need to feel happy and balanced, which strengthens trust and respect.

Boundaries help define where one partner ends and the other begins, outlining what they are comfortable with and where they draw the line. This clarity is essential as it prevents misunderstandings and ensures that both partners feel respected and valued. For instance, you might set a boundary around personal time, specifying that certain hours of the day are meant for self-care or personal hobbies. Effectively Communicating this need involves expressing its importance to your well-being and the relationship's health. These boundaries must be respected once set, as consistent respect reinforces trust and understanding, allowing both partners to feel secure in both their individuality and their relationship.

The concept of interdependence offers a robust framework for understanding how balancing independence and intimacy can coexist harmoniously. Interdependence occurs when partners mutually depend on each other while maintaining their autonomy. This dynamic allows both individuals to feel emotionally connected and supported without feeling the need to sacrifice their independence. Achieving independence requires open communication about each partner's needs and a commitment to support those needs. It involves creating a partnership where both individuals contribute to and benefit from the relationship equally, fostering a sense of teamwork and mutual respect.

Navigating the space between closeness and personal space can sometimes feel like navigating a complex labyrinth, where turning one corner too sharply can lead to walls rather than open doors. The key here is communication and flexibility. Discuss with your partner how much closeness and space each of you needs and understand that these needs might change depending on circumstances like stress at work or personal issues. It's essential to approach these discussions without judgment, recognizing that needing space does not indicate a lack of love or commitment. For instance, one might need an evening alone to decompress after a particularly stressful day. Communicating this need respectfully ensures that it is not misinterpreted as a rejection. Similarly, expressing a desire for more closeness, perhaps wanting to spend more time together during the weekend, should be seen as an opportunity to strengthen the bond, not as a demand or imposition.

By embracing these strategies, you create a relationship dynamic that honors both the 'I' and the 'We.' This balance cultivates a healthier, more satisfying relationship and supports personal growth and happiness. As you and your partner continue to navigate this delicate balance, you'll find that your relationship becomes a source of strength and freedom, a safe harbor where individuality and togetherness are both celebrated and cherished.

7.4 Transforming Jealousy into Compersion

Understanding jealousy in relationships is like navigating through a maze of emotions, where fears and insecurities lurk in unexpected corners. Jealousy often springs from a deep-seated fear of loss or a perceived threat to the relationship, triggering protective instincts that can inadvertently strain connections. These reactions, though meant to safeguard love, sometimes backfire, creating a cycle of doubt and mistrust. To break free from this cycle, it's essential to confront the underlying insecurities that fuel jealousy, often rooted in past experiences of abandonment or betrayal. Recognizing that these feelings stem more from internal fears than external threats is a crucial first step in reshaping how we respond to triggers of jealousy.

Enter compersion—a refreshing antidote to jealousy. The concept of compersion, which can be seen as the antithesis of jealousy, involves feeling joy and contentment in your partner's happiness with others. Originating from non-monogamous communities, compersion is a mindset that celebrates the independent sources of happiness in your partner's life, be it friendships, hobbies, or other relationships. It's a radical shift from viewing these aspects as threats to seeing them as enriching elements that contribute to your partner's well-being and, by extension, to the health of your relationship. Embracing compersion starts with self-reflection and a sincere assessment of your values and security within the relationship. It requires an understanding that love is not finite but can expand and manifest in multiple forms and connections.

Several steps can be instrumental in cultivating compersion and mitigating jealousy. First, engaging in open and honest communication about your feelings of jealousy is crucial. This discussion should not be accusatory but rather exploratory, aiming to understand each other's perspectives and emotional triggers. Here, active listening plays a crucial role as it helps validate feelings and fosters empathy. Secondly, building trust through transparency and consistency in actions and assurances can reassure the anxious partner that their emotional and relational needs are being met. Another effective strategy involves setting realistic and mutually agreed-upon boundaries that respect personal spaces yet foster closeness. These boundaries should be flexible and may need periodic adjustments as the relationship grows and evolves.

A practical exercise to facilitate the transition from jealousy to compersion involves journaling about instances when you felt jealous. Detail the situation, your feelings, and how you reacted. Then, reflect on how compersion could have altered your perception and response. Consider what would need to change in your mindset or emotional state to feel compersion in similar future situations. This reflective practice can highlight patterns in your emotional responses and help cultivate a more compersive outlook over time.

Case Study: Alex and Jamie

Alex and Jamie, a couple who struggled with Alex's jealousy due to Jamie's close friendships with others, provide a real-life example of transforming jealousy into compersion. Alex, who had experienced betrayal in a past relationship, found it challenging to not feel threatened by Jamie's external connections. Through couples therapy, they worked on understanding Alex's triggers and communicated openly about each other's needs and boundaries. Jamie ensured transparency about their interactions with friends and consistently reassured Alex of their commitment.

Over time, Alex began to engage in activities that built self-esteem and personal contentment outside the relationship, which was pivotal in reducing the reliance on Jamie for emotional validation. They also started a ritual where they shared aspects of their day that brought them joy, fostering a shared space of happiness and appreciation. Gradually, Alex began to experience joy in Jamie's happiness with friends, seeing how these relationships contributed positively to Jamie's life and, consequently, to their relationship.

This shift wasn't overnight but evolved through consistent effort, communication, and a commitment to understanding each other's perspectives.

By celebrating love in all its forms and focusing on the enrichment brought into their lives through diverse experiences and connections, Alex and Jamie transformed their relationship into one marked by security and mutual joy. This case exemplifies how embracing cooperation, supported by trust and open communication, can effectively diminish the impact of jealousy, leading to a more fulfilling and secure relationship.

7.5 Attachment and Physical Intimacy: Navigating the Complexities

Physical intimacy and attachment styles intertwine in ways that profoundly affect the dynamics of any close relationship. Understanding this connection is crucial, especially when considering how the varying levels of comfort and anxiety associated with different attachment styles can influence physical closeness and expression of affection. For individuals with secure attachment, physical intimacy is often a robust source of comfort and connection, a way to express love and receive reassurance of their partner's affection. Conversely, those with anxious attachment might find that their need for physical closeness stems from a place of insecurity, a need to seek validation of their partner's feelings for them through constant physical contact. This can sometimes overwhelm their partners, creating a dynamic that might actually feed into the anxieties fueling their behavior.

Addressing issues in physical intimacy that stem from anxious attachment begins with open communication. It's essential to have honest discussions about each partner's comfort levels and expectations regarding physical intimacy. This conversation should be approached with sensitivity and without judgment, allowing each person to express their needs and fears openly. For example, if one partner needs more physical closeness than the other is comfortable giving, they need to discuss ways to meet in the middle that respect both of their boundaries. Therapy can be an invaluable tool in these discussions, particularly with a therapist specializing in attachment issues, who can provide guidance tailored to addressing these specific dynamics. Such therapists can help individuals understand how their attachment style influences their behavior and needs, offering strategies to cope with and gradually adjust these patterns. This personalized approach ensures that the therapy does not adopt a one-size-fits-all methodology, which might not be effective for everyone, especially those with nuanced experiences and personal histories related to attachment.

Building a secure and satisfying physical connection with your partner goes beyond simple physical contact; it involves creating an environment where both partners feel safe and valued. This safety is fostered by mutual respect and understanding of each other's physical and emotional boundaries. It's essential to regularly check in with each other's feelings and comfort levels, making adjustments as needed. For instance, initiating physical contact can be a mutual agreement rather than a unilateral action, ensuring both partners feel comfortable and willing at that moment. Practices such as asking for consent before initiating intimacy, even in long-term relationships, reinforce respect and consideration, strengthening the trust and emotional connection that form the basis of a secure attachment.

The role of non-sexual affection in building and maintaining a secure attachment bond cannot be overstated. Simple gestures like holding hands, a casual touch as you pass by each other in your home, or a comforting hug can significantly reinforce the bond between partners. These acts of affection are crucial in daily interactions as they reaffirm the physical and emotional connection between partners, providing constant, subtle reassurances of love and commitment. They play a vital role in creating a continuous sense of presence and availability, which is particularly comforting to individuals with anxious attachment styles. By integrating such gestures into everyday interactions, partners can cultivate a habit of expressing love and care, which acts as a steady foundation for the relationship, reassuring both partners of their bond and significantly easing anxieties related to attachment.

Navigating the complexities of physical intimacy and attachment styles requires patience, understanding, and a willingness to adapt and grow together. By fostering open communication, seeking appropriate therapeutic support, respecting mutual boundaries, and regularly engaging in acts of non-sexual affection, partners can build a secure, satisfying physical connection. This connection enhances their relationship and contributes to their overall emotional and psychological well-being.

7.6 The Power of Shared Growth: Evolving Together

Adopting a growth mindset within the context of a relationship means embracing the idea that both partners can evolve and develop together, continuously enhancing and deepening their connection. This perspective is crucial because it shifts the focus from a static understanding of each other's capabilities to a dynamic one, where change and growth are not only expected but encouraged. By fostering a growth mindset, you view challenges and disagreements not as insurmountable problems but as opportunities for learning and mutual development. This approach helps maintain a positive and resilient relationship, even in the face of difficulties.

Shared goals and dreams act as a compass that guides your relationship through the complexities of daily life. When you and your partner set goals together—whether they're financial, such as saving for a home or personal, like committing to health and fitness—you create a shared vision that fosters unity and teamwork. This collaborative process involves discussing what each of you wants to achieve, finding common ground, and supporting each other's individual aspirations that contribute to this shared vision. For instance, if you dream of buying a home, you might set shared financial goals and individually contribute by managing personal spending or taking on extra work. Such shared endeavors strengthen your partnership by aligning your efforts and reinforcing your commitment to each other.

Supporting each other's personal growth is equally important and can significantly enhance the resilience and depth of your relationship. This support can take various forms, from encouraging each other to pursue new interests or career opportunities to providing emotional support during personal challenges. It's about celebrating each other's successes and being there during failures, providing a stable and supportive base from which both of you can confidently explore personal ambitions. For example, if your partner decides to go back to school, you might take on more household responsibilities to help ease their stress. Supporting each other in such tangible ways not only strengthens the relationship but also builds a deep sense of gratitude and loyalty between partners.

Celebrating achievements together is a joyful and bonding experience that reinforces the strength of your partnership. Whether it's a promotion at work, a personal project completed, or simply sticking to a new fitness regime, taking time to celebrate these victories together can greatly enhance the feeling of teamwork and shared success. It's about acknowledging that each individual's success benefits the relationship as a whole, creating a culture of appreciation and mutual respect. These celebrations can be as simple as a special dinner out, a thoughtful gift, or a surprise party with friends. The act of celebration not only shows that you value and take pride in each other's accomplishments but also deepens your connection by creating shared moments of joy and satisfaction.

As you integrate these strategies into your relationship, you cultivate a dynamic where growth and support are woven into the fabric of your partnership. This dynamic not only enriches your personal lives but also ensures that your relationship remains strong, adaptable, and deeply satisfying. As you continue to evolve together, you'll find that your relationship becomes a source of strength and inspiration, a true partnership that enhances every aspect of your life.

Thriving Beyond Anxious Attachment

In a quaint suburban neighborhood, Sarah sat on her porch, sipping her morning coffee as she watched the sunrise. The past year had been a journey of transformation for her. After years of struggling with anxious attachment, Sarah had decided to take charge of her emotional well-being. She had immersed herself in self-help books, attended therapy sessions diligently, and leaned on a supportive network of friends who understood her journey.

One crisp autumn afternoon, Sarah received an unexpected invitation from an old friend, Emily, whom she hadn't seen since college. Emily had always been the adventurous type, while Sarah tended to shy away from unfamiliar situations. Despite her initial hesitation, Sarah agreed to meet Emily at a local café.

As they settled into a cozy corner of the café, Emily noticed the subtle change in Sarah's demeanor. "You seem different, Sarah. In a good way," Emily remarked with a warm smile.

Sarah chuckled softly, feeling a mixture of pride and vulnerability. "I've been working on myself a lot lately. Trying to break free from old patterns."

Emily nodded knowingly. "I get that. Remember our college days? You were always so cautious, and I was the risk-taker."

Sarah smiled, recalling their contrasting personalities back then. "I guess some things never change, huh?"

Their conversation flowed effortlessly as they caught up on each other's lives. Emily shared stories of her recent travels and new experiences, while Sarah listened intently, admiring her friend's courage. Eventually, the topic turned to more personal matters.

"I've been reading about anxious attachment and how it affects relationships," Emily confessed, her voice softening. "It made me reflect on my own patterns."

Sarah's heart skipped a beat. Here was someone who understood the struggles she had faced—the sleepless nights, the constant need for reassurance, the fear of abandonment. "I know exactly what you mean," Sarah admitted, her voice tinged with vulnerability. "It's been a tough journey, but I'm learning to navigate it."

Emily reached across the table, squeezing Sarah's hand gently. "You're stronger than you think, Sarah. Look how far you've come."

Their conversation deepened as they shared insights from their respective journeys. Emily talked about the importance of continuous communication in her relationships, while Sarah opened up about her challenges in adapting to change. They exchanged tips on seeking support when needed and reflected on their personal growth through journaling and celebrating milestones.

As the afternoon sun began to fade, Sarah felt a sense of gratitude for this unexpected reunion. Emily's presence had been a reminder that growth and healing were ongoing processes, not solitary endeavors. Together, they discussed their visions for the future, of creating secure attachments and passing on emotional resilience to future generations.

———

Overcoming anxious attachment is a journey - much like climbing a mountain. The landscape behind you is marked with the signs of your resilience and commitment to growth. Yet, the path ahead unfolds with new landscapes to explore and further heights to achieve. This chapter is about consolidating the gains you've made in overcoming anxious attachment and ensuring that these changes are not just for today but are ingrained into your life, enabling you to thrive in all of your relationships.

8.1 Maintaining Your Progress: Strategies for Long-Term Success

Continuous Communication

Communication is the lifeline of any relationship. It needs to be open, honest, and ongoing. For those who have battled with anxious attachment, keeping communication channels clear is vital to prevent misunderstandings and insecurities from festering. Regular check-ins with your partner about your feelings, needs, and concerns help to maintain the health of your relationship. Discuss your progress and the areas you still need to work on openly.

Encourage your partner to share their thoughts and feelings as well. This bi-directional communication ensures that both partners are on the same page and can support each other effectively. It's not just about talking through issues as they arise but also about sharing moments of joy and success, strengthening the bond and reinforcing your relationship's positive dynamics.

Adapting to Change

Change is a constant in life, and adapting to it is vital for any relationship to thrive. Your relationship must adapt to reflect these changes as you and your partner grow and evolve. This might mean renegotiating your needs, adjusting your boundaries, or finding new ways to support each other. Embrace these changes as opportunities to deepen your connection and learn more about each other. For instance, if a new job requires one partner to travel frequently, discussing ways to maintain closeness and manage separations effectively is crucial. It might involve setting routines for daily check-ins or creating special rituals for reconnecting after time apart. Adapting to changes also means celebrating each other's growth and seeing each individual's evolution as a strength that they bring to the relationship.

Seeking Support When Needed

No matter how much progress you've made, there might be times when you need external support. Recognizing when you need help and seeking it proactively is a sign of strength and self-awareness. This could mean revisiting a therapist when you feel old patterns emerging or joining a support group to connect with others who are navigating similar challenges. Therapists, support groups, or relationship coaches can provide you with insights and tools that are invaluable in maintaining your progress. They offer a perspective outside of your immediate relational environment, which can be crucial for overcoming blind spots and continuing on your path of growth. Don't hesitate to reach out for professional help when you feel overwhelmed or stuck. It's an investment in your well-being and the health of your relationships.

Reflection Journal Prompt

To aid in ongoing self-reflection, consider maintaining a reflection journal. Here's a prompt to get you started: Write about a recent situation in your relationship where you felt old anxieties creeping in. How did you handle it? What strategies did you use that helped? What could you do differently next time? Reflecting on such questions regularly can enhance your self-awareness and help cement the coping strategies that work best for you.

As you continue to navigate your path, remember that each step you take is not just about moving away from anxious attachment but moving toward a richer, more connected, and fulfilling relational life. Each effort, each strategy, and each support you seek is a building block in creating a legacy of love and security, not just for yourself but for all your current and future relationships.

8.2 When to Seek Professional Help: Signs and Signals

Sometimes, despite your best efforts, the emotional landscape you navigate might feel too complex or overwhelming to manage alone. Recognizing when to seek professional help is a crucial step toward continued growth and healing, particularly when dealing with the intricacies of attachment issues. Signs that you might need to reach out for professional guidance often manifest as persistent feelings of unhappiness or anxiety in your relationships that don't seem to improve despite your self-help efforts. You might find yourself repeatedly falling into the same patterns that strain your relationships despite having gained insights and tried to change on your own. Other indicators include experiencing intense emotional reactions that seem disproportionate to the situation at hand or when your worries about your relationships start to interfere significantly with your daily life, work, and well-being.

Therapy, whether individual or couples, offers a structured environment where you can explore the deeper roots of your attachment issues with the guidance of someone who understands the complexities of human emotions and relationships. There are numerous benefits to seeking professional help. A therapist can help you identify and change underlying thoughts and behavioral patterns more effectively than you could on your own. They can provide tools and strategies tailored specifically to your needs, accelerating your growth. Moreover, therapy offers a safe space to explore painful emotions and traumatic experiences that might be the source of your attachment issues, facilitating more profound healing that might be difficult to achieve without professional help.

Choosing the right therapist is critical to the success of your therapeutic journey. It's important to look for a qualified professional and a good fit for your personality and therapeutic needs. Start by seeking a therapist who specializes in attachment theory and relationship dynamics. They will have a deeper understanding of your issues and can offer insights and interventions that are specifically effective for attachment-related problems. You might also want to consider their therapeutic approach—whether it's more structured or more exploratory, and what kind of therapy they offer, such as cognitive-behavioral therapy, psychodynamic therapy, or others. It's also beneficial to have an initial consultation with a potential therapist to see if you feel comfortable with them and to discuss your goals for therapy. This step ensures that you and the therapist clearly understand what you hope to achieve and can work together effectively.

Combining therapy with personal efforts like reading self-help books, attending workshops, and engaging in self-care practices can create a comprehensive approach to overcoming your attachment issues. While therapy provides professional insights and strategies, your personal efforts help reinforce what you learn in therapy and apply it in real life. This combination can lead to more sustained and profound growth, as you are receiving guidance and actively integrating and practicing new skills in your day-to-day life. Engaging in activities that promote self-awareness and emotional health, such as mindfulness practices, journaling, or attending relationship workshops, complements the therapeutic work by continuously nurturing your growth and adaptation outside of the therapy sessions. This holistic approach enhances your resilience, equipping you with many tools to manage your attachment style and improve your relationships effectively.

8.3 The Role of Support Networks in Healing Attachment Wounds

A robust support network can act like a safety net as you navigate the difficulties of transforming attachment styles. Imagine you are at a climbing gym, tackling a challenging wall. Below you, a group of fellow climbers watches, ready to offer advice, cheer you on, and hold your rope taut. Just like these climbers, a network of supportive friends, family, and peers becomes invaluable as you work toward secure attachment. This network comprises individuals who understand the nuances of your emotional landscape and provide emotional, intellectual, and sometimes physical support as you navigate through your healing process.

Building this support network requires intention and mindfulness. It starts with identifying the people in your life who are empathetic, understanding, and knowledgeable about emotional growth—or at least willing to learn. These might be friends who have shown an interest in personal development, family members who have always offered a listening ear, or peers who are also on their own paths of emotional healing. It's essential to nurture these relationships regularly; just as plants need water to thrive, so do your relationships need time and attention. Engage with these individuals regularly, share your progress, discuss your setbacks, and listen to their experiences. This mutual exchange strengthens your bonds and provides a well-rounded perspective on handling emotional challenges, enriching your journey toward secure attachment.

Furthermore, community resources play a pivotal role in expanding and reinforcing your support network. Many communities offer support groups and workshops that focus on building secure attachments and managing attachment disorders. These groups provide a platform to meet others who are facing similar challenges, allowing for the exchange of stories, strategies, and support. Online forums and social media groups can also be valuable resources, offering access to a broader community of individuals engaged in similar journeys. These platforms often provide anonymity, which can make it easier to share personal experiences and insecurities. Engaging with these communities can validate your feelings, provide encouragement, and introduce you to new ideas and strategies that others have found helpful. It's like having a map that shows multiple paths others have taken to climb similar peaks, giving you options and insights into your journey.

The healing power of sharing cannot be understated. Opening up about your experiences in a safe space can catalyze profound healing and growth. Sharing allows you to externalize your thoughts and emotions, seeing them more clearly and often understanding them better. It can also break the isolation that often comes with dealing with attachment issues, as you realize others share similar struggles. This act of vulnerability typically fosters deep connections with others, providing emotional relief and a sense of belonging. Moreover, as you hear others share their stories, you gain different perspectives and strategies that might resonate with your situation, providing practical solutions and hope.

However, while building and engaging with your support network, it's crucial to maintain healthy boundaries. This ensures that your interactions support your growth and do not inadvertently reinforce dependency or old patterns of anxious attachment. Setting boundaries with others might involve defining how often you engage with them, the types of support you are comfortable receiving, and how you want to handle feedback. It's about communicating your needs clearly and respectfully, ensuring that the support offered aligns with your personal growth and autonomy goals. For instance, you might appreciate a friend checking in on you but prefer that they do so weekly rather than daily. Or, you might find certain topics too sensitive to discuss in a group setting and like to talk about them in one-on-one situations or with a therapist. Establishing these boundaries will help you feel secure and respected in your interactions, fostering a support system that genuinely contributes to your healing and growth.

As you continue to weave these support threads into your life, remember that each conversation, shared experience, and boundary set shapes a stronger, more resilient fabric of relationships. This network supports you today and becomes a part of your ongoing growth, a testament to the power of community and connection in healing and transforming attachment wounds.

8.4 Celebrating Your Growth: Acknowledging Milestones

Acknowledging the milestones in your path toward secure attachment and healthier relationships is a powerful affirmation of your progress. It's akin to placing markers along a hiking trail, each representing a point where you paused, looked back, and realized how far you've come. These milestones could be as significant as feeling no anxiety when your partner is out of contact for a day or as subtle as choosing a calm conversation over an anxious reaction during an argument. Recognizing these moments is crucial because it provides a sense of accomplishment and reinforces your capability to change and grow. Celebrating these milestones involves more than just a mental acknowledgment. Creating a tangible record —perhaps through journal entries, a dedicated calendar, or even a creative visual board—can be a daily reminder of your journey and progress. Each entry acts as a beacon of your resilience and commitment, encouraging you continually on days when the path seems steep.

Creating personal or shared rituals to celebrate this progress can significantly enhance the sense of achievement and joy in your journey. These rituals can be deeply personal and reflective, like a quiet evening reviewing your journal and reflecting on your growth, followed by a self-reward such as a favorite meal or a special purchase. Alternatively, they could be shared—perhaps a monthly 'celebration dinner' with your partner or a close friend where you discuss the past month's growth and challenges, celebrating both the ups and downs as integral parts of your progress. Such rituals make self-improvement more enjoyable and weave your growth into the fabric of your everyday life, making it a lived experience rather than just an abstract goal. They transform your milestones from personal victories into shared joys, enhancing your relationships through shared experiences of growth and achievement.

Gratitude for the journey, including the challenges that have spurred growth, plays a transformative role in how you perceive your path to secure attachment. Each obstacle overcome and each lesson learned contributed to your current state of resilience and emotional intelligence. Regularly expressing gratitude for these experiences, through gratitude journaling or meditative practices, can shift your focus from what was painful to what was gained from those experiences. This shift is not about denying the difficulty of past experiences but about reframing them as valuable lessons that contributed to the strength and wisdom you hold today. Such a perspective fosters a deeper appreciation for your journey, enhancing your emotional and psychological well-being.

Sharing your success stories with others offers a dual benefit: it not only reinforces your sense of accomplishment but also inspires and guides those struggling with similar issues. Consider sharing your journey in support groups, online forums, or even in casual conversations. When you vocalize your challenges and how you overcame them, you not only validate your own experiences but also provide hope and practical guidance to others. This act of sharing can be incredibly empowering, as it often leads to a reciprocal exchange of stories and strategies, broadening your understanding and support network. Moreover, hearing others' stories of overcoming anxious attachment can provide new insights and reinforcement, reminding you that you are not alone in this, that transformation is possible, and that your efforts are part of a larger narrative of growth shared by many.

As you continue to navigate your path, remember that each step forward, each challenge embraced, and each milestone celebrated deepens your journey toward a life characterized by secure attachments and fulfilling relationships. These celebrations are not just markers of where you've been but beacons lighting the way forward, illuminating your path with the knowledge that change is possible, progress is achievable, and the capacity for growth resides within you.

8.5 Creating Your Future: Life Beyond Anxious Attachment

Envisioning a future where secure attachment is the norm rather than the exception in your relationships begins with a clear, intentional mental image of what such relationships look like. This vision acts as a compass, guiding your decisions and interactions toward healthier dynamics. Picture yourself in scenarios where trust, mutual respect, and emotional support are abundantly present. Imagine responding to relationship stresses with a calm and constructive approach, feeling deeply connected to your partner even during disagreements. This practice of visualization is not just fanciful thinking; it's a proven psychological tool that helps align your subconscious mind with your conscious goals, making it easier to adopt behaviors that foster secure attachments. To solidify this vision, write detailed descriptions of a day in your ideal relationship. Include how you communicate, resolve conflicts, and support each other. Revisit and revise this vision as you grow and learn, allowing it to evolve as you do.

Setting realistic, achievable goals is the next step in making this vision a reality. Start by identifying specific behaviors you want to change or develop. For instance, if maintaining calm during conflict is part of your vision, a related goal might be to practice mindfulness daily to improve your emotional regulation. Break down these goals into small, manageable steps to start implementing immediately. If your goal is to enhance trust in your relationship, one step might be to share small, personal experiences with your partner daily, gradually building intimacy. Keep track of these goals in a journal or an app designed for goal management, and review them regularly to assess your progress and make adjustments as needed. Remember, the key to successful goal-setting is flexibility; allow yourself the space to modify your goals as you discover what works best for you and your relationships.

Maintaining optimism and hope, especially during setbacks or challenges, is crucial in your journey toward secure attachment. Challenges are inevitable, but they don't have to derail your progress. When faced with setbacks, try to view them as opportunities for learning and growth rather than failures. Maintain a solution-focused mindset, asking yourself, "What can I learn from this situation?" and "How can I handle this better next time?" Keeping a 'challenge journal' where you record both the challenge and your response can help you see patterns in handling difficulties and track your growth over time. Additionally, engaging in activities that boost your mood and outlook can be incredibly beneficial. Whether it's a hobby you enjoy, exercise, or spending time in nature, make time for activities that rejuvenate your spirit and reinforce your resilience.

Lifelong learning and growth in the context of relationships and personal development are about remaining open and curious about yourself and your partner. It involves continuously seeking knowledge about healthy relationship dynamics, communication skills, and emotional intelligence. Attend workshops, read books, or even take courses on topics related to relationships and psychology. This commitment to learning keeps you engaged with the latest ideas and practices that can enhance your relationships. It also helps you stay adaptable, a key quality in maintaining healthy relationships. Encourage your partner to join you in this educational journey, making learning a shared activity that in itself strengthens your bond. This shared commitment to growth not only enriches your relationship but also keeps it dynamic and evolving, ensuring that both partners are actively engaged in nurturing its health and vibrancy.

As you continue to build your future with secure attachments at its core, remember that every small step you take is a significant leap toward a life of richer, more fulfilling relationships. These efforts shape not just your interactions with others but how you view and value yourself and your capacity to love and connect.

8.6 Legacy of Love: Passing on Secure Attachment to Future Generations

The influence we wield on the next generation, particularly in how they form and maintain relationships, is profound and far-reaching. By instilling the principles of secure attachment in our children and future generations, we actively contribute to breaking cycles of insecure attachment that may have pervaded our families for years. This proactive approach not only enhances the emotional well-being of our children but also enriches the fabric of society by fostering individuals who are capable of forming healthy and fulfilling relationships. Consider the child who grows up in an environment where emotions are expressed openly, and relationships are built on trust and mutual respect. This child learns to view the world as a safe place, where emotional expression is not just accepted but encouraged, and where relationships are reliable sources of support and comfort.

Modeling healthy relationships is one of the most effective ways to teach children about love, respect, and secure attachment. Children are keen observers, often mimicking the behaviors they see in their parents and primary caregivers. When they witness healthy communication, respect for boundaries, and supportive partnership, they internalize these patterns as the norm for their own future relationships. For instance, consider a scenario where a child sees their parent apologizing after a disagreement. This simple act shows that disagreements are a natural part of relationships and teaches the child the importance of reconciliation and taking responsibility for one's actions. Similarly, when children see their parents supporting each other during times of stress or celebrating each other's successes, they learn the value of empathy, support, and mutual respect in relationships.

Open communication about attachment and emotional health is crucial and should be tailored to be age-appropriate. Starting conversations about feelings and relationships early in a child's life helps to normalize emotional expression and teaches them to identify and articulate their feelings. These discussions can start simply, with questions like, "How did it make you feel when...?" and responses that validate their feelings, such as, "It's okay to feel sad/angry/happy about that." As children grow, these conversations can evolve to include more complex aspects of relationships and attachment styles. Educating children about the different ways people can relate emotionally can empower them to navigate their own relationships more effectively and make sense of the behaviors of those around them. Additionally, such discussions can foster resilience, as children learn that while they may not always have control over what happens, they do have a choice in how they respond emotionally.

Creating a secure family environment is foundational to fostering healthy attachments. This environment is characterized by stability, safety, and open lines of communication. It is an environment where family members know that their feelings and thoughts will be met with understanding and respect. Establishing such an environment involves consistent routines, clear expectations, and fair rules that are enforced with love and respect. It also means creating a space where family members can express their emotions without fear of judgment or reprisal. Activities that strengthen the family bond, such as regular family meals, game nights, or even family meetings to discuss plans and issues, can reinforce a sense of unity and belonging. In such an environment, children develop a secure base from which they can explore the world, confident in the knowledge that they have a safe and supportive space to return to.

In ensuring that the legacy we pass on is one of love and secure attachment, we do more than just influence our immediate family; we contribute to the generational transmission of emotional health and relational well-being. This legacy is not just about avoiding the pitfalls of insecure attachment but about actively fostering an environment where future generations can thrive emotionally and relationally. By embedding the principles of secure attachment in our familial and community interactions, we set the stage for a future where healthy, fulfilling relationships are the norm, not the exception.

As we conclude, remember that each step you take toward fostering secure attachment in your family and community plants the seeds for healthier future generations. These efforts are an investment in a legacy of emotional and relational health that will pay dividends far beyond your immediate family, contributing to a society where individuals are equipped to build and maintain fulfilling relationships. As we shift our focus from personal growth to communal influence, let's commit to nurturing love, respect, and security in all our relationships, paving the way for a future rich in emotional connection and mutual support.

Conclusion

As we approach the finish line of this wild adventure together, let's pause for a moment and marvel at how far we've come. We began by diving headfirst into the world of anxious attachment—discovering its origins and the sneaky ways it can interfere with our relationships. Along the way, we've dug up some simple yet powerful tools and gained insights on the practical ways we can heal and grow. This book has been your trusty guide, leading you through the maze toward more secure attachments and a happier emotional state.

We began by dissecting the anatomy of anxious attachment, recognizing how deeply embedded these patterns can be, stemming from our earliest interactions. Through the chapters, we learned not only to identify the signs of anxious attachment in ourselves and our interactions but also the profound importance of self-awareness and emotional regulation. We delved into practical strategies like mindfulness, setting healthy boundaries, engaging in meaningful inner child work, and embracing the healing power of self-compassion.

But this journey isn't just about romantic relationships—it's about transforming every facet of our lives because anxious attachment impacts every aspect of our lives from our emotional well-being, to our self-esteem, and interactions with friends, family, and colleagues. Secure attachments form the bedrock upon which we can build a life of emotional fulfillment and resilience.

But remember, the closing of this book is not the end of your journey. Keep growing, keep learning. Consider it a stepping stone, an invitation to continuous growth and learning in your personal and relational development. Stay curious and proactive, applying the strategies that resonated most with you and gradually incorporating more tools as you grow more confident in your path to healing.

I urge you to take concrete steps today. Choose one or two practices we discussed that felt particularly impactful, and commit to integrating them into your daily routine. As you become more comfortable, expand your toolkit, always moving at a pace that honors your personal journey.

Remember the importance of your support network in moments of doubt or challenge. Whether it's friends, family, support groups, or professionals, reaching out for help is a profound strength, not a weakness. These resources can provide invaluable support and insight as you navigate the complexities of anxious attachment.

Let my story be a beacon of hope for you. As someone who has walked this path, I assure you that overcoming anxious attachment is not only possible—it's achievable with persistence, self-compassion, and the right strategies. You have the power to transform your relationships and live with greater security and confidence.

As we part ways in this book, I leave you with this final thought: "Your journey toward secure attachment and fulfilling relationships begins with a single step of self-awareness and self-love. Embrace your journey with courage, and remember, you are not alone." Let this message guide you as you continue to forge paths of connection, understanding, and profound love in all your relationships.

Now that you've absorbed the tools to trust others fearlessly, transcend childhood wounds, and nurture the robust relationships you desire, it's your turn to pay it forward and illuminate the path for fellow seekers.

By sharing your authentic thoughts about this book on Amazon, you're not just leaving a review; you're signaling to others where they can discover the insights they seek. Together, we can extend a lifeline to more individuals striving to break free from the grip of anxious attachment once and for all.

Thank you for your invaluable contribution. Each review you leave shines a light of hope, guiding others toward the transformative journey you've embarked upon. Your generosity in sharing your experiences is instrumental in fostering healing and growth in countless lives.

Simply scan the QR code below to leave your review and thank you for joining me on this journey.

References

Ackerman, C. E. (2018). What is attachment theory? Bowlby's 4 stages explained. Positive Psychology, 27

Ackerman, C. E. (2018). What is self-regulation? (+95 skills and strategies). Positive Psychology

Agishtein, P., & Brumbaugh, C. (2013). Cultural variation in adult attachment: The impact of ethnicity, collectivism, and country of origin. Journal of Social, Evolutionary, and Cultural Psychology, 7(4), 384–405

Arancibia, M., Lutz, M., Ardiles, Á., & Fuentes, C. (2023). Neurobiology of disorganized attachment: A review of primary studies on human beings. Neuroscience Insights, 18, 1–10

Arancibia, M., Lutz, M., Ardiles, Á., & Fuentes, C. (2023). Neurobiology of Disorganized Attachment: A Review of Primary Studies on Human Beings. Neuroscience Insights, 18, 263310552211456. https://doi.org/10.1177/26331055221145681

Baltimorepsych. (2023, June 16). Anxious Attachment Style In Romantic Relationships Explained. Northern County Psychiatric Associates. https://www.baltimorepsych.com/anxious-attachment-style-in-relationships

Cassidy, J., & Shaver, P. R. (Eds.). (2008). Handbook of attachment: Theory, research, and clinical applications (2nd ed.). The Guilford Press

David, S. (n.d.). Susan David - Home. Susan David. Retrieved May 27, 2024, from http://www.susandavid.com

Eddins Counseling Group. (n.d.). DBT mindfulness exercises to regulate emotions

Gulli, L. (2024, February 6). Attachment Theory - When It's Helpful and When It's Not. Choose Recovery Services. https://www.chooserecoveryservices.com/attachment-theory-when-its-helpful-and-when-its-not/

Guy-Evans, O. (2024). Anxious attachment style: Signs in adults, how it develops & how to cope. Psych Central

Harper, C. (n.d.). How to Build a Support System For Your Mental Health. Mywellbeing.com. https://mywellbeing.com/therapy-101/how-to-build-a-support-system

Hilgers, M. (n.d.). Anxious Attachment Style Therapy. Michael Hilgers, M.MFT. Retrieved May 27, 2024, from https://michaelhilgerslpc.com/anxious-attachment-style/

Holland, K. (2020, June 27). Positive Self-Talk: Benefits and Techniques. Healthline. https://www.healthline.com/health/positive-self-talk

Jacob, A. and A. (2016, September 30). Conflict is a Normal and Natural Part of Your "Happily Ever After." The Gottman Institute. https://www.gottman.com/blog/conflict-normal-natural-part-happily-ever/?

Jill. (2017, November 9). Managing vs. Resolving Conflict in Relationships: The Blueprints for Success. The Gottman Institute; The Gottman Institute. https://www.gottman.com/blog/managing-vs-resolving-conflict-relationships-blueprints-success/

Johnson, S. M., & Greenman, P. S. (2006). The path to a secure bond: Emotionally focused couple therapy. Journal of Clinical Psychology, 62(5), 597–609. https://doi.org/10.1002/jclp.20251

Levine, A., & S.F. Heller, R. (2018). Compatibility Quiz | Attached the Book. Attached the Book. https://www.attachedthebook.com/wordpress/compatibility-quiz/?step=1

Moore, C. (2019, June 2). How to practice self-compassion: 8 techniques and tips. Positive Psychology. https://positivepsychology.com/how-to-practice-self-compassion/

Noor, S. (2022, March 10). Tips to help with an anxiety attack. Retrieved from https://shireennoor.com/2022/03/10/tips-to-help-with-an-anxiety-attack/

Nguyen, J. (2024, May 9). How to Heal an Anxious Attachment Style, According to a Relationship Coach. Verywell Mind. https://www.verywellmind.com/how-to-heal-an-anxious-attachment-style-8643714

Nguyen, J. (2024). How to self-soothe anxious attachment: A guide. Briana MacWilliam

Noor, S. (2022, March 10). Tips to Help With an Anxiety Attack. Wh51591.Webhealersites2.com. https://www.shireennoor.com/2022/03/10/tips-to-help-with-an-anxiety-attack

Reid, S. (2023, March 1). Setting healthy boundaries in relationships. Help Guide. https://www.helpguide.org/articles/relationships-communication/setting-healthy-boundaries-in-relationships.htm

Robinson, L. (2024, February 5). Effective Communication. Help Guide. https://www.helpguide.org/articles/relationships-communication/effective-communication.htm

Rusnak, K. (2022, March 9). The Importance of Vulnerability in Healthy Relationships | Psychology Today. Www.psychologytoday.com. https://www.psychologytoday.com/us/blog/happy-healthy-relationships/202203/the-importance-vulnerability-in-healthy-relationships

Schewitz, D. S. (2023, December 22). How to Rebuild Trust After Betrayal. Couples Learn. https://coupleslearn.com/rebuild-trust-after-betrayal/

Scott, E. (2022, January 25). How to improve your relationships with effective communication skills. Verywell Mind. https://www.verywellmind.com/managing-conflict-in-relationships-communication-tips-3144967

Shaver, P. R., & Mikulincer, M. (2009). An overview of adult attachment theory. In J. H. Obegi & E. Berant (Eds.), Attachment theory and research in clinical work with adults (pp. 17–45). The Guilford Press

Sutton, J. (2021, November 9). Conflict Resolution in Relationships and Couples: 5 Strategies. PositivePsychology.com. https://positivepsychology.com/conflict-resolution-relationships/

Sutton, J. (2021, July 6). How to Perform Assertiveness Skills Training: 6 Exercises. PositivePsychology.com. https://positivepsychology.com/assertiveness-training/

Tatkin, S. (2012). Wired for Love. New Harbinger Publications.

Team. (2021, December 21). The Power of Forgiveness: 6 Tips on How to Let Go of the Past. Attachment Project. https://www.attachmentproject.com/blog/the-power-of-forgiveness-6-tips-on-how-to-let-go-of-the-past/

Victoriainnerchildwork. (2022, November 9). 12 Powerful Inner Child Healing Exercises to Reclaim Your Inner Child - Inner Child Work. Innerchildwork.co.uk. https://innerchildwork.co.uk/12-powerful-inner-child-healing-exercises-to-reclaim-your-inner-child/

Wimberger, L. (n.d.). What Is The Definition Of Neuroplasticity